COUNTER-REVOLUTION

JAN ZIELONKA

COUNTER-REVOLUTION

Liberal Europe in Retreat

OXFORD
UNIVERSITY PRESS

OXFORD
UNIVERSITY PRESS

Great Clarendon Street, Oxford, OX2 6DP,
United Kingdom

Oxford University Press is a department of the University of Oxford.
It furthers the University's objective of excellence in research, scholarship,
and education by publishing worldwide. Oxford is a registered trade mark of
Oxford University Press in the UK and in certain other countries

First Edition published in 2018

Impression: 1

Published in the United States of America by Oxford University Press
198 Madison Avenue, New York, NY 10016, United States of America

British Library Cataloguing in Publication Data
Data available

Library of Congress Control Number: 2017953263

ISBN 978-0-19-880656-1

Printed in Great Britain by
Clays Ltd, St Ives plc

ACKNOWLEDGEMENTS

This letter greatly benefited from the thoughtful comments of numerous colleagues and friends. Stefania Bernini, Neil Dullaghan, and Martin Krygier have read and improved each page of this long letter and I am particularly grateful to them. Special thanks go to Iradj Bagherzade, Jaroslava Barbieri, Christopher Bickerton, Franck Düvell, Michael Freeden, John Keane, Giuseppe Laterza, Paul Nolte, Loukas Tsoukalis, Herman Van Gunsteren, Jacek Żakowski, and three anonymous reviewers. I also benefited from frequent exchanges with graduate students in European Politics and Society at the University of Oxford. Last but not least I would like to thank Dominic Byatt and his colleagues from Oxford University Press for steering this project to the intended destination in a wholehearted and professional manner.

CONTENTS

PROLOGUE

Several months after the fall of the Berlin Wall Ralf Dahrendorf wrote a book fashioned on Edmund Burke's *Reflections on the Revolution* in France.[1] Like Burke, he chose to put his analysis in the form of a letter to a gentleman in Warsaw.[2] The intention was to explain the extraordinary events taking place in Europe. Dahrendorf did not share Burke's liberal conservatism and his book does not read like Burke's political pamphlet. Dahrendorf tried to reflect calmly from his study at St Antony's College in Oxford on the implications of the turbulent period around 1989. He saw a liberal revolution evolving in Eastern Europe and he tried to identify opportunities that this revolution created as well as possible traps lying in its path.

My book is written in the form of a letter to Ralf, my late German mentor. It follows Dahrendorf's line by trying to reflect on the implications of the equally turbulent period three decades later. I see an illiberal counter-revolution developing in Europe and I aim to understand its roots and implications. Is Europe disintegrating? Can open society survive? How is the economic crisis to be overcome? Will Europeans feel secure again?

Although Dahrendorf's and my books are written in the same spirit and in the same location they are nevertheless quite different. I may well hold the title of Ralf Dahrendorf Professorial Fellow, but I am not Ralf Dahrendorf, of course. He grew up in fascist Germany; I grew up in communist Poland. His adult life witnessed states developing the welfare system, parliaments regulating markets, and the printed press being the key site of democratic discourse. My adult life witnessed states dismantling welfare systems, parliaments de-regulating markets, and the internet being the key site of democratic discourse. Dahrendorf was a member of the political establishment ('albeit a maverick one'[3]): a German minister, a British Lord, and a European Commissioner. I also moved between different countries, but remained a kind of 'intellectual provocateur' with no political affiliations or functions.[4]

Most importantly, our books deal with opposite processes. His book talks about the revolution opening borders for people, ideas, and trade, about constructing the rule of law and democracy, about overcoming the ghosts of Westphalia in interstate relations, while my book talks about the counter-revolution destroying all that. His book is about extending the liberal project into Eastern Europe; my book is about the retreat of this project under pressure from anti-liberal insurgents all over the continent.

This is not a book on populism, however. This is a book about liberalism. Populism has become a favourite topic within liberal circles and no one has ever exposed populist deceptions and dangers better than liberal writers. Yet, liberals have proved better at finger-pointing than at self-reflection. They spend more time explaining the rise of populism than the fall of liberalism. They refuse to look in the mirror and recognize their own shortcomings, which led to the populist surge across the continent. My book intends to address this imbalance; this is a self-critical book by a lifelong liberal.

When Dahrendorf wrote his book there was a lot of confusion in Europe, but uncertainty was chiefly confined to its eastern part where the communist system had begun to crumble. Today, the entirety of Europe is in a state of confusion, with the liberal system beginning to crumble not just in Warsaw and Budapest, but also in London, Amsterdam, Madrid, Rome, Athens, and Paris. Europe's citizens feel insecure and angry. Their leaders look incompetent and dishonest. Their entrepreneurs seem frantic and distressed. Political violence is on the rise, chiefly because of terrorism, but not just. How is it possible that a peaceful, prosperous, and integrated continent is falling apart? Why did seemingly pragmatic Europeans embark on a journey into the unknown under populist banners? Why is Europe's economic governance neither just nor effective? Who or what should be blamed? How shall we survive the current turmoil? And, most crucially, how is the pendulum of history to be reversed? These are the questions I will be wrestling with here.

My letter suggests that Europe and its liberal project need to be reinvented and recreated. There is no simple way back. Europe has failed to adjust to enormous geopolitical, economic, and technological changes that have swept the continent over the past three decades. European models of democracy, capitalism, and integration are not in sync with new complex networks of cities, bankers, terrorists, or migrants. Liberal values that made Europe thrive for many decades have been betrayed. The escalation of emotions, myths, and ordinary lies left little space for reason, deliberation, and conciliation.

Another 'valley of tears' is therefore ahead for Europeans, because I don't think that either Chancellor Merkel or President Macron will single-handedly get Europe out of the current predicament. However, liberalism may be down, but it is not out. The neo-liberal detour has done much damage, but there is no reason to abandon some core liberal credos: rationality, liberty, individuality, controlled power, and progress. The counter-revolutionaries have made many gains by exploiting pathologies of the EU, liberal democracy, and the free market, but they lack a plausible programme of recovery and renewal.

Europe has many dark chapters in its history, but it also has bright ones showing a remarkable capacity for intellectual reflection, public deliberation, and institutional innovation. I strongly believe that the current European predicament could well turn into another wonderful renaissance, but this will require serious reflection on what went wrong. This letter attempts this reflection without prejudice and dread.

I am a political analyst, not a philosopher or historian. I try to understand how certain political ideas shape strategies of political and economic entrepreneurs. Typologies and the evolution of various liberal streams are better analysed somewhere else. Unlike most historians, I look back to understand, if not envisage, the future. By pointing to various novel features of democracy, economics, and communication I try to suggest a new liberal project for a continent challenged not only by the counter-revolutionary 'earthquake', but also by gradual technological, societal, and environmental processes. This letter is partly about modernity, connectivity, and digitalization. How is it possible to make states, cities, regions, and international organizations perform better in an ever more interdependent environment? How can transparency, accountability, and governmentality be enhanced in a Europe with 'fuzzy' borders? How shall citizens be protected from violence, exploitation, and climate change? How is the politics of fear to be replaced with the politics of hope? At times I may sound exceedingly gloomy in this letter, but I believe in a happy ending for Europe and even for liberals.

1

FROM REVOLUTION TO COUNTER-REVOLUTION

Dear Ralf,

Several hours after the Brexit referendum results were announced students and tutors from your St Antony's College gathered in the European Studies Centre. Most of those present, a pretty international crowd, were depressed, some even had tears in their eyes. They could not believe that the majority of British voters opted for leaving the European Union. They could not understand why a mountain of rational arguments in support of the remain vote fell on deaf ears. Why was a vast body of statistical evidence showing the costs of leaving the EU ignored? How could seemingly pragmatic Brits refuse to trust them: the academics, the journalists, the experts? And why had shady politicians such as Nigel Farage, Andrea Leadsom, and Michael Gove prevailed over the winners of recent parliamentary elections, David Cameron and George Osborne? Most of these questions remained unanswered.

Just before the Brexit referendum I was in Italy where the Five-star movement led by a comedian, Beppe Grillo, won control over Rome and Turin in local elections. In Rome the social democratic administration has been accused by the Five-star movement of nepotism, incompetence, and corruption. The election results were an unexpected blow to the leader of the Democratic Party, Prime Minister Matteo Renzi. Stunned Italian commentators were bluntly told by Grillo: 'You are unable to comprehend the birth and rise of my movement because you are translating everything into your own language. You are simply cut off from reality.'[1] A few months later

Matteo Renzi stepped down as Prime Minister after failing to win a majority for his constitutional reforms in a referendum.

After the Brexit referendum I flew to Poland where opposition parties accused the winner of the previous year's elections of orchestrating a constitutional coup, paralyzing the judiciary system, and purging public media of suspected critics. 'I am not a dictator,' Jarosław Kaczyński told daily *Rzeczpospolita*. 'Poland is an example of democracy and an island of liberty in a world where freedom is in short supply.'[2]

What is going on? Who is wrong and who is right? How does one establish truth in this era of post-truth? Have European voters gone insane? Are Nigel Farage, Beppe Grillo, and Jarosław Kaczyński prophets or frauds? Do these three above-mentioned political experiences have something in common? Do they show a new development in European politics, and if so, how do we name it?[3] We clearly live in turbulent times with highly uncertain outcomes. Long-standing assumptions do not hold any longer. Symbolic politics has taken over from real politics. Everything seems possible at present. And yet, we need to make sense of the history rolling over Europe with a force and pace unknown since you wrote *Reflections on the Revolution in Europe* nearly three decades ago.

Let me return to your concerns and put the current developments in the context of the 1989 Revolution that you examined. I do so because I believe that we are witnessing a concerted effort to dismantle the system created after the fall of the Berlin Wall. We are witnessing a counter-revolution.

What happened in Great Britain on 23 June 2016 is only one of many episodes heralding the rise of a powerful movement aimed at destroying the narrative and order that dominated the entire continent after 1989. Under attack is not just the EU but also other symbols of the current order: liberal democracy and neo-liberal economics, migration and a multicultural society, historical 'truths' and political correctness, moderate political parties and mainstream media, cultural tolerance and religious neutrality. As the cited Italian, British, and Polish cases show, there are local variations of this movement, but the common denominator is the rejection of people and institutions that have governed Europe in the last three decades. Moreover, let's not delude ourselves by pointing to the results of the 2017 elections in the Netherlands, France, and the United Kingdom. Mark Rutte, Emmanuel Macron, and Theresa May have embraced some of the counter-revolutionary rhetoric to win the popular vote. Rutte castigated migrants, Macron bashed traditional parties, and May embraced a hard Brexit. Can liberalism survive with so many illiberal ornaments? Should liberals rejoice because soft populists prevailed over hard ones? Even in prosperous and stable Germany, the right-wing nationalist Alternative for Germany (AfD) entered the Bundestag with nearly a hundred seats in the 2017 elections. Angela Merkel remained in power, but her party and social democratic allies suffered a historic defeat.

We should also consider the broader geopolitical context. Illiberal politicians are ruling with the voters' blessing in Europe's two largest neighbours, Turkey and Russia. The election of Donald Trump as President of the United States of America also has grave implications for the old continent. The US may well be separated from Europe by the Atlantic, but the US is a quintessential European power; no major decision is taken in Europe without America in mind. Donald Trump talks like many European counter-revolutionaries and when running for the presidency he was publicly endorsed by such prominent European insurgents as Marine Le Pen and Nigel Farage.

The Meaning of Change

Why is this a counter-revolution? There are neither barricades raised on European streets nor sit-in strikes in factories. There is no particular ideology inspiring and uniting protest movements. There is much talk about anti-politics, but those who lead the protest create parties and try to win elections. Yet, it would be a mistake to assume that revolution or counter-revolution must always involve mass mobilizations and violence culminating on a certain date.

Communism collapsed with little if any violence. Poland's Solidarity movement was able to organize mass strikes in 1980, not a decade later. Change came chiefly through pacts between old and new elites and through elections. And yet it is hard to deny that this relatively peaceful process changed Europe beyond recognition. History did not end, but the old order has gradually been replaced by a new one. Although some of the former communists were able to stay in power, they were able to do so only after endorsing the new liberal order. This is why you rightly called it a revolution despite all qualifications. And, since you wrote your book in 1990, the revolution has greatly progressed.

The Soviet Union and Yugoslavia disintegrated, Germany has been reunited and the European Union as well as NATO have been vastly expanded. Western armies, laws, firms, and customs moved eastward. Many people enthusiastically welcomed new regimes in their territory, but some felt disadvantaged either because of their ethnic background (e.g. Russians in Latvia, Serbs in Bosnia-Herzegovina) or because they lacked adequate professional skills to function in the new competitive environment. A long-standing balance of power in Europe has been effectively reshuffled. Russia soon began to see herself as an underdog, but also France found herself in a weaker position vis-à-vis Germany than was the case before.

Geopolitical revolution has been followed by economic revolution. With the fall of communism some of its more universal ideals came under fire: collectivism, redistribution, social protection, and state intervention in the economy. This paved the way for neo-liberal economics to assume a dominant position throughout the entire continent, not just in Great Britain. Deregulation, marketization, and privatization became the order of the day even in states run by socialist parties. The private sector has subsequently expanded at the expense of the public sector. Markets and market-values moved into spheres that used to be the domain of the public sector in Europe such as health, education, public safety, environmental protection, and even national security. Social spending has been contained if not slashed altogether for certain disadvantaged groups. Even in countries such as France or Spain, once home to powerful unions, less than 10 per cent of the workforce is unionized now. Membership of Poland's Solidarity trade union has fallen fivefold since 1989. Today less than 5 per cent of Poland's workforce is unionized.

Across Europe, politics was increasingly presented as an art of institutional engineering and not as an art of political bargaining between the elites and the electorate. More and more powers were delegated to non-majoritarian institutions—central banks, constitutional courts, regulatory agencies—to make sure that reason rather than passion guides political decisions. Politics giving in to public pressure was considered irresponsible if not dangerous. Majorities were said to spend money they didn't have, to discriminate against all kind of minorities, to support such ethically knotty causes as the death penalty or torture. Citizens were to be educated rather than listened to. The notion that public interests need to reflect public wishes has been questioned. Interests were said to be best identified by experts: generals, bankers, traders, lawyers, and, of course, leaders of the ruling parties.

The EU with its enlarged powers following the 1991 Maastricht Treaty has been a prototype of a non-majoritarian institution led by 'enlightened' experts largely independent from electoral pressures. True, the European Council consisted of democratically elected politicians, but the introduction of majority voting has made it difficult for member states to veto some decisions. In fact, national executives proved eager to bypass their respective parliaments by making decisions in the European Council.

Historians may question my periodization. Liberal ideals have influenced different generations of politicians since the Age of Enlightenment. Parties which formally called themselves liberal had more power before 1989 than after.[4] Neo-liberal economics had been on the rise in Western Europe for a number of years before the fall of the Berlin Wall. The liberal type of democracy was born in Eastern Europe in 1989, but in Western Europe it was born much earlier. That said, 1989 represented a symbolic triumph of liberal ideals. With the fall of the Berlin Wall liberalism became 'the only game in town' across the entire continent. Post-communist states have become the most enthusiastic advocates of neo-liberal economics. They also embraced the process of European integration with the greatest fervour. Different streams of liberalism merged into a single pan-European ideological project; formerly distinct political groupings of the centre-left and centre-right have united under the liberal banner; the liberal order has been embraced in such distant geographic locations as Lisbon, Helsinki, and Bucharest. In this sense, the liberal revolution has indeed been built on the ruins of the Berlin Wall, even though history does not end or begin on any particular date.[5]

Targets of Contestation

You, Ralf, may find my description of liberal rule over the past three decades too harsh and one-sided. Yet, unless you assume that the insurgents have divine powers of deception, it is hard to explain why voters began to desert the liberal cause.[6] Something must have gone very badly wrong, don't you think?

The legacy of the past three decades is not only negative, of course. The Soviet system was inefficient, unjust, and oppressive; there is no reason to be nostalgic about its demise. Neo-liberal economics proved able to generate growth and innovation. And the dangers of a majoritarian politics acting with no constitutional or fiscal constraints are real. Why should a government of the day be allowed to create debts that have to be repaid by the next generations of taxpayers? Its democratic mandate, however strong, relates to the current, not the future generation of electors. And if the winners of elections try to curb the rights of religious minorities or the rights of women, should this be allowed?

Even the opaque democracy in the EU can be defended. As Robert A. Dahl rightly argued, larger units are obviously further away from their citizens, but they are in a better position to cope with global pressures for the sake of their citizens. There is an important trade-off between citizens' participation and system effectiveness.[7]

However, this is a rather generous evaluation of the post-1989 order and does not take into account power politics. Each revolution produces winners and losers; the latter ought to be accommodated in some way or else they rebel. Satisfying losers is never easy. West Germany has invested a huge sum of money in East Germany, but despite all the investments some citizens in the eastern part are still resentful about the post-1989 changes. They may be free and affluent at present, but they feel like second-class German citizens. Clearly, accommodating losers is not only about money. Poland has grown more than any European country over the past decade, yet in 2015 the majority of Poland's electorate supported a counter-revolutionary party campaigning on an anti-liberal and anti-European ticket. They found the elite successfully ruling Poland more interested in the opinion of international rating agencies, foreign press, and European bureaucrats than in that of their own ordinary citizens. Warnings that this regime change would generate dire political and economic consequences were ignored.

Most other parts of Europe have not done so well economically as Germany and Poland, which obviously made it easier for the critics of the (neo-)liberal revolution to thrive. Consider, for instance, Hungary where the combination of weak state capacity, incompetent economics, and corruption paved the way for an authoritarian, if not autocratic, leader such as Viktor Orbán. Portugal, Greece, and Spain found themselves insolvent following the 2008 global financial crisis. With GDP plunging and unemployment sky-rocketing it was obviously impossible to keep everybody happy. Those dependent on the shrinking public provisions, those with no skills to compete in the market, or those squeezed by mobile migrant labour were ready to switch their vote to political entrepreneurs who opposed the dominant order. Even relatively affluent countries such as Italy, France, Austria, Holland, Denmark, Sweden, and Finland have found it difficult to avoid pressure coming from anti-establishment parties.

The Euro crisis and the subsequent refugee crisis demonstrated that the new order is less effective and liberal than claimed by its proponents. 'Post-capitalism' and 'post-democracy' are clearly inferior to the original brand.[8] The two crises also highlighted the growing imbalances among individual states of Europe. There are not only creditor states and debtor states, but also decision-makers and decision-takers. Some even talk about a German (accidental) empire in Europe.[9] Moreover, the two crises showed that European leaders are unable to reverse their course and adopt more effective actions. Strict rules of the Fiscal Compact Treaty left virtually no space for indebted countries to adjust their economic policies and there is no agreement on how to handle migration in a humane and effective manner.

The case of Greece is very illustrative here. Greece is no longer allowed to take sovereign socio-economic decisions, but the policies imposed on it by fellow Europeans are clearly not working. After three successive and expensive bailouts there is little hope that Greece will ever repay its debts. Nor is it credible to claim that Greece will effectively control its borders after numerous EU summits telling Greece what ought to be done. No wonder the handling of Greece has disappointed many Greeks whose views were ignored after the 2015 referendum and the 2014 elections. Frustrated also are the voters in countries effectively ruling Greece because they clearly are not getting proper returns on their investments.

When faced with the electoral pressure from the 'new kids on the block' the established right- and left-wing parties chose to jump into bed together rather than admitting past mistakes and reversing their policies. We witnessed such previously unimaginable alliances as those between the conservative New Democracy and socialist PASOK in Greece and between Berlusconi's Forza Italia and the post-communist Democratic Party in Italy. This only reinforced the impression that old ideological dividing lines are gone and have been replaced by a new (neo-)liberal notion of normality or, if you wish, rationality. The official narrative became black and white. The establishment insisted on continuing with projects that gave Europe 'prosperity and peace' and it accused critics of trying to undermine its noble efforts. Self-reflection, let alone self-criticism, have been missing.

The EU was proclaimed to be the engine of cooperation and those who criticized it were called agents of Putin. The fact that the EU has recently generated major conflicts by mishandling the Euro crisis, the refugee crisis, and to some extent also the crisis in Ukraine has been ignored or denied. Basic facets of neo-liberal economics were still treated as sacrosanct even though this type of economics contributed to the financial bubble of 2008 and caused hardship for millions of Europeans. Nor was there an acknowledgement that the existing system of parliamentary representation needs to be fundamentally rethought. Curbing the powers of central banks, constitutional courts, the EU, and other non-majoritarian institutions has not been seriously contemplated, let alone orchestrated by the mainstream parties.

With the passage of time, unsolved problems started to mount and the official rhetoric became more aggressive. Questioning the established taboos was portrayed as irresponsible if not insane. The rulers were prepared to offer some cosmetic concessions to an ever more desperate electorate, but so far no serious plan B has been proposed by the winners of the 1989 revolution. The electorate has been remarkably patient for some time, but it has slowly started to desert the established parties. This has opened a window of opportunity for alternative politicians. They have promised that a change of a government would mean a genuine change of policies if not the existing system altogether.

The Counter-Revolutionary Insurgents

The counter-revolutionary politicians represent a very mixed bag. They include such diverse characters as Marine le Pen, Beppe Grillo, Matteo Salvini, Geert Wilders, Gerolf Annemans, Alice Weidel, Alexander Gauland, Christian Thulesen, Jimmie Akesson, Timo Soinini, Norbert Hofer, Nigel Farage, Viktor Orbán, Jarosław Kaczyński, Robert Fico, Andrej Babis, Alexis Tsipras, and Pablo Iglesias. Their personal backgrounds and ideological roots are very different: from neo-fascist to neo-communist, from libertarian to conservative, from anti-austerity to anti-Muslim, from nationalist to secessionist. Some are moderate, while others are hardliners. Those who managed to take control of their countries talk and act differently from those who are still campaigning from the sidelines. However, they all have one thing in common: they are against the order installed after the 1989 revolution. They attack not only those who ruled Europe after 1989, but also their key political projects: European integration, constitutional liberalism, and neo-liberal economics.

Migrants have been at the centre of political campaigns for most of the counter-revolutionary insurgents, because migrants represent a quintessential product of the post-1989 policy of opening borders, of protecting minorities, and of forging economic interdependence. Some of these politicians may well be racists,[10] but there is no evidence to suggest that xenophobia is the main reason for their anti-immigration stance. I consciously excluded from the above counter-revolutionary list of politicians those who are primarily driven by ethnic hatred, such as Ilias Panagiotaros of the Greek Golden Dawn Party and Gabor Vona of the Hungarian Jobbik Party.

Of course, throwing into one bag such diverse politicians as Jarosław Kaczyński and Alexis Tsipras is problematic. The former is ultra-conservative, while the latter is radically leftist. Kaczyński sees Russia as a threat, while Tsipras sees Russia as an ally. Kaczyński wants to soften the nasty edge of neo-liberalism, while Tsipras is fundamentally opposed to neo-liberal economics. Kaczyński would like the EU to be more detached and intergovernmental, while Tsipras would like the EU to be more compassionate and federal. Kaczyński is wholeheartedly against accepting refugees, while Tsipras is calling for a just and effective system of reallocation of refugees. And yet, it is difficult to deny that both Kaczyński and Tsipras loathe the elites that ruled their countries for the past decades and they both aspire to transform their respective countries in a fundamental way. They make concessions when pressed by such powerful figures as Angela Merkel or institutions such as the EU or the IMF, but this does not mean that they are giving up their struggle for a fundamentally new regime in their respective countries.

The counter-revolutionary politicians are often called populist. This term is misleading and stigmatizing and fails to identify the key objective of these politicians, namely the abolition of the post-1989 order and replacement of the elites associated with this order. I find numerous statements of these politicians highly objectionable, but this does not mean that their critique of the current order is not valid, at least in some part. The ruling political and intellectual elite is all too keen to call all kinds of critique 'populist'.

Populists are said to propose simple solutions to complicated problems. However, there is nothing wrong with simple solutions if they are just, efficient, and adopted according to democratic procedures. The minimum wage and inheritance tax represent widely used, simple solutions for coping with complex inequality problems. Should they be called 'populist' and therefore abandoned? Populists are said to use moralistic rhetoric, make unrealistic promises, and launch unfair personal attacks on their opponents. Sadly, all these characteristics can be attributed to most current politicians and not just to the group discussed here. Ahead of all national elections politicians from different parties make empty social promises. Bombastic and moralistic rhetoric is also part of the liberal repertoire. Consider the 'axis of evil' rhetoric on the eve of the 2003 Iraq invasion. Smearing political foes is a routine part of all political campaigns. Consider the way the liberal intellectuals and politicians describe their 'populist' opponents. A meeting between Nigel Farage and Julian Assange in March 2017 was compared to a Hitler–Stalin pact by Nick Cohen in *The Guardian*.[11] Farage, according to Cohen, 'exploits chauvinism and plays on racial fears', while Assange 'provides support services to the gangster capitalists of the new Russian empire'. 'Extremes merge. Red bleeds into black,' concluded Cohen. I guess the author of this article sees himself not as a populist, but as a liberal.

Populists are said to overemphasize the cleavage between 'the elite' and 'the people'; the former is being demonized and the latter idealized. In their view, politics should be an expression of the *volonté générale* of the people.[12] The people may not be as 'pure' and 'sensible' as populists claim; likewise, the elite may not be as 'corrupted' and 'inefficient' as they assert. Yet, the distinction between the people and the elite is quite legitimate, and democracy should make sure that the former have some control over the latter. This is not to endorse a plebiscitarian notion of democracy, but to argue for democracy that is responsive to electoral wishes and that gives the electorate meaningful means of changing the elites in power and their actual policies.

Margaret Canovan once pointed out that democracy has two facets: redemptive and pragmatic. The former sees the people as the only source of legitimate authority and promises salvation through the policy of popular mobilization. The latter sees democracy as a form of government with institutions limiting power and making it effective. Populists are trying to emphasize the former aspect and to exploit the gap between the promise and performance of democracy.[13] Is this such a deplorable strategy, I wonder.

Of course, much depends on the details. Populists often use an extremely hard language appealing to the dark side of human instincts in defiance of the recognized moral and political norms.[14] In fact, this is their purposeful strategy. Challenging the notion of established normality requires crossing the border of political correctness.[15] Liberals may find it morally disgraceful and aesthetically displeasing. They may portray 'the ugly others' as irresponsible and dangerous. I don't deny that there are often legitimate grounds for such portrayals. Yet, those 'others' are increasingly more skilful at winning elections. As Simon Jenkins put it succinctly in the *Guardian*: 'Those others are not "populist"—the latest buzzword of intellectual abuse—they are just popular.'[16] In the summer of 2017 the counter-revolutionary insurgents were already running a government in Hungary, Poland, Slovakia, and Greece. They were part of a government in Finland, and were propping up a minority government in Denmark. In Italy the Five-star movement and in the Netherlands the Party for Freedom were the main opposition parties, while in France the 'populist' candidate came second in the presidential elections, defeating leaders of all other established parties. In Great Britain 'populists' were able to carry the day in the Brexit referendum and gained ground in both leading parties, Tories and Labour. In the Autumn of 2017, the Euro-sceptic ANO party of the billionaire Andrej Babis won the parliamentary elections in the Czech Republic, and the elections in Austria and Germany recorded notable achievements of right-wing 'populists' from the FPÖ and AfD parties.

The last case shows that the counter-revolutionary influence can hardly be measured by electoral performances only. They set the tone of the political discourse and establish which issues are debated; they give voice to people's anxieties and expose liberal flaws; they arouse the politics of fear, acrimony, and vengeance. Nigel Farage was not even able to win a seat in the British parliament, and yet it is hard to overestimate his impact on the result of the Brexit referendum. The fact that mainstream liberal parties in France were not able to put forward a strong enough candidate to challenge Marine Le Pen is also telling. I am happy to give Emmanuel Macron the benefit of the doubt, but he is still a rather mysterious political entrepreneur: an ex-banker rising to political prominence through the Socialist Party which he then betrayed to form his own political movement, *En Marche!* (Forward!), which he defines as neither left nor right.[17] When Macron won the Presidential election, Italian newspapers labelled him a savior of Europe, but several weeks later some of them accused him of declaring war on Italy and European principles. This is because Macron refused to help Italy cope with refugees, broke a deal with the Libyan rival leaders without consulting Italy, and nationalized a French shipyard to avoid an Italian take-over.

Self-proclaimed liberals have also progressively adopted rhetoric that resembles the populist one by any standards. This was most striking on the eve of the Dutch elections in 2017. In order to see off the threat of Geert Wilders, the Liberal Party (VVD) adopted 'a strategy that could have come from President Trump's playbook', to cite the *New York Times*.[18] In his victory speech the VVD leader, Mark Rutte, declared that the Dutch voters had put a halt to 'the wrong kind of populism', implying that there is a good and a bad kind of populism, the former represented by himself, and the latter by Wilders.[19] VVD's coalition partner, the Christian Democratic Party (CDA), has also entertained a nationalist and anti-immigration rhetoric. In the new Dutch parliament, MPs representing hard and soft populist parties have an overwhelming majority. The Labour Party, which led the Dutch government for most of the past three decades, has seen its parliamentary representation virtually wiped out; they have only nine MPs now. In 2012 they won thirty-eight seats, in 1998 forty-five seats, and in 1989 forty-nine seats. A similar decline of the liberal left is progressing in many other countries of Europe. The most striking example is Poland where no single left-wing liberal was able to win a parliamentary seat in the 2015 elections.

Traditional parties, especially on the right, not only entertain illiberal rhetoric and policies, but they also form political alliances with those whom they call populists. This happened first in 2000 in Austria when the Austrian People's Party formed a government with Jörg Haider's Freedom Party of Austria. Silvio Berlusconi ruled Italy with the help of *Lega Nord* and after the 2015 elections the Finns Party entered coalition government with two centrist parties. These coalitions between soft and hard 'populists' have not led to the death of the latter, but blurred the difference between the two groups. Some soft populists became hard populists in time. Poland's PiS party and Hungary's Fidesz party are good examples. The Italian *Lega Nord* has been transformed from a soft populist separatist movement into a fully-fledged populist movement imitating the French *Front National*. That said, the main cleavage and contest in contemporary Europe is not between soft and hard populists. The real contest is between the winners of the post-1989 revolution and those who intend to topple them and dismantle the post-1989 system. The latter may well be 'populist,' they may form tactical alliances, they may be neo-nationalists or post-Marxists, but they are first of all counter-revolutionaries with a mission.

This probably also applies to Jeremy Corbyn, who took over the leadership from the liberal wing of the Labour party with a programme reminiscent of the pre-1989 or even pre-1968 era. Corbyn has unmasked major flaws of the liberal revolution without questioning some of the core liberal principles. Tories and Blairites label Corbyn a populist, but his views on migration, minority rights, parliamentary democracy, and foreign intervention are less populist than those of his critics. Corbyn's programme may be unsuited for tackling modern transnational economics, but his focus on inequalities, workers' rights, and the predatory behaviour of financial services can hardly be called illiberal. One can even argue that Corbyn has shown traditional liberal parties the way to get out of the current gridlock. However, I should quickly add that Corbyn does not call himself a liberal and does not strive for a liberal renaissance. In this sense, he is a counter-revolutionary, albeit of a special kind.

Identifying Priorities

Destroying the existing order is one thing and constructing a new one is another. Contemporary counter-revolutionary forces know better what they are against than what they are for. Details of their current agendas do not form a coherent whole, and they are pretty vague. Those who studied the party manifestos of counter-revolutionary movements concluded that they allow a lot of room for statements on everyday political matters that may not always be consistent with the mainstream party line.[20] Moreover, each of the counter-revolutionary movements has its own local priorities that would be difficult to bring into one line in a broader European context. Marine Le Pen works closely with Geert Wilders, for instance, but not with Jarosław Kaczyński, Nigel Farage, or Alexis Tsipras.

More crucially, the record of counter-revolutionary forces in office is disquieting, to put it mildly. In Poland the centre-right liberals from the PO party may well have failed to make the public media free from political interference, but the PiS counter-revolutionary party has transformed these media into a propaganda arm of its fundamentalist faction. The Greek counter-revolutionary Syriza party promised to correct the wrongdoings of the past, but has instead attempted to introduce a media licensing law that would reward their political cronies. This attempt has been halted by the Greek constitutional court, something which could not happen in Poland where the PiS party paralysed the constitutional court immediately after coming to power. Both PiS in Poland and Syriza in Greece have also tried to appoint their political associates to all important (and even unimportant) positions within the civil service. They both tried to gain control of publicly owned enterprises and even private banks, albeit with no signs of reversing neo-liberal policies. Both PiS and Syriza progressively embraced a nationalist agenda blaming Europe for all their own shortcomings.

The counter-revolutionaries have not behaved any better in other countries. The Italian Five-star movement won the 2016 election for the city council in Rome, but the first few months of its reign was characterized by remarkable chaos and incompetence even by poor 'Roman' standards. Above all, there is a long, disturbing, and ever-growing list of autocratic policies by the Hungarian party Fidesz. Senator John McCain has even called their famous leader a 'neo-fascist dictator'.[21]

All these and other flaws of counter-revolutionary parties should not make the established parties complacent, however. There is hardly any evidence suggesting that the 'liberal' policies of the last two or three decades are back in vogue among Europe's electorate. If the established parties are able to hold onto power, it is because they progressively embraced illiberal rhetoric and policies.[22] True, Alexander Van der Bellen won the 2016 Austrian presidential elections without trying to water down the liberal agenda, but his uncompromising stance was uncommon and his victory was narrow and hard fought. One should also ask the question 'how could Norbert Hofer, a politician with an extreme-right background, be so close to the presidential office in one of the most affluent and stable European countries?' The counter-revolutionary forces are far from conquering the entire continent, but they are able to shape the public discourse and push the established parties into a frenzied retreat. This is not because insurgents have an inspiring programme and charismatic leadership. This is chiefly because the liberals are doing so badly.

Have liberals lost the plot or is my description somewhat preju-diced? Perhaps I am too hard on liberals and too lenient on the counter-revolutionary forces. I am a convinced liberal like you, Ralf, and I am deeply concerned about the rise of illiberal politics. As a 'child' of the 1989 liberal revolution I do not want to see civil liberties being curbed again, the rule of law dismantled, media freedom strangled, and walls reappearing across the continent. That said, I am not interested in entertaining a nostalgia for the lost era of liberal glory. The proponents of the liberal propaganda of success ought to ask themselves a simple question: if the last three decades of liberal rule was such a great accomplishment, why have so many people started to hate liberals?

We need to understand what liberalism is and what it is not. We need to decide which streams of liberalism we want to refute and which to support. For the last three decades, liberalism was an ideol-ogy of power and empowering; everything was liberal in some sense; questioning liberal principles was uncommon; even former commun-ists jumped on the liberal train together with ordinary opportunists hoping to advance their careers. I feel little in common with these liberal fellow travellers. I want to understand what we could have done better and I have no intention of concealing our mistakes. Only after serious self-reflection would we be able to conclude if liberalism is worth fighting for. This is in line with the famous imperative of Socrates, to 'know thyself'.

I have big problems with liberals castigating 'populists' and then behaving suspiciously similarly. I take issue with liberals switching from noble public schemes to backroom manipulation. You may say that I have a naive vision of politics. Does everyday politics not require compromises? Is it not better to support a lesser evil? My normative reply is as simple as the pragmatic one. Soft forms of 'populism' do not belong to the liberal repertoire, however defined, and they proved self-defeating in political practice. This does not mean that there is only one sacred and non-negotiable dogma that we can proudly call liberalism. Nor does it mean that all varieties of liberalism are worth fighting for. This means only that bashing the counter-revolutionary forces on its own is not likely to lead to the liberal renaissance. If the counter-revolutionary forces are doing well because liberals are doing so poorly we need first of all to address the liberal failings. This letter is therefore about healing or re-inventing liberalism.

In 1963 Karl Popper, one of the leading liberal intellectuals, identified two contrasting attitudes in the field of politics:

> The first is that of the politician who thinks that all he does is well done, and that none of our troubles are due to his mistakes, but, rather, to unavoidable misfortunes, or to the conspiracies of his opponents, who are bad men. The opposite attitude is that of the man who, aware of his fallibility, knows that he is bound to err; who is constantly on the watch for his own mistakes, because he knows that this is the only way to learn, and profit, from experience; and who hopes that his opponents, by their criticism, will help him discovering [*sic*] his mistakes.[23]

Popper found the latter attitude more appropriate for liberals like himself. I follow his dictum in this letter.

2

WHY THEY HATE LIBERALS

For liberals like you and me, Ralf, it is tempting to believe that liberalism is a force for good that the evil counter-revolutionaries are determined to destroy. Like all humans, we make mistakes and at times we fail to live up to our ideals. Yet, the comparison between us and our anti-liberal opponents seems crystal clear: we are rational, they are illogical if not crazy; we tell the truth, they tell lies; we offer progress, they offer destruction; we are open-minded, they are intolerant; we enhance freedom, they seek domination; we believe in laws and institutions, they are trying to get rid of them. If people support the counter-revolution they must be either brain-washed or mad.

This description is too biased, I fear. As intellectuals we should not entertain Manichean black and white thinking. As democrats we should not ridicule electoral choices. As public activists we should not delude ourselves that people will suddenly 'wake up' and rally behind us once again. Voters had legitimate reasons to desert liberal politicians and their parties. Yet, our liberal friends are more eager to engage in finger-pointing than to acknowledge their own shortcomings and mistakes. Have liberals betrayed their ideals, and if so, which ones and how? Are the deficiencies of liberalism accidental mistakes or structural flaws in the liberal doctrine? Perhaps some of the liberal principles proved unfeasible or even erroneous. Perhaps elitism, inequality, dysfunctional parliaments and European institutions, even hedonism and greed are the products of liberalism. Perhaps liberalism has a naive take on human predispositions and power politics. If some of this is correct we should say 'sorry' and apologize for deceiving the electorate. Perhaps we should renounce liberalism altogether, or at least some of its aspects.

This negative narrative is probably too harsh, but we will know the answers to the preceding questions only after a serious self-critical, if not soul-searching, analysis. Our conclusions are not likely to be straightforward. This is partly because, as Michael Freeden pointed out, 'Liberalism supplies one of the numerous maps available as people attempt to navigate through their social and political environments.'[1] Socialism and conservatism offer competing but not mutually exclusive maps. Karl Popper's advocacy of 'piecemeal' rather than 'holistic social engineering' would be endorsed by most conservative politicians or people, for instance. Most liberals would affirm the socialist quest for progress and social justice. Leszek Kołakowski even proposed a *ménage à trois*—Conservative-Liberal-Socialism.[2]

This leads to another complication; liberalism does not represent a single coherent phenomenon as portrayed and demonized by its contemporary critics. To cite Martin Krygier, 'Liberalism is a broad church' with a long 'laundry list of "liberal" commitments'.[3] Krygier also talks about liberalism with adjectives.[4] Conservative liberals have little in common with social democratic ones; neo-liberals have been accused by classical liberals of usurping the term 'liberals' for a very narrow, and broadly conservative/capitalist, doctrine. Both Friedrich von Hayek and Karl Popper may well be seen as quintessential liberal thinkers, but their respective views are quite contrasting, as you rightly pointed out, Ralf.[5]

In short, when we talk about successes and failures of liberalism we need to specify which type of liberalism we are talking about. We should also distinguish between liberalism in government and liberalism in society. Institutional liberalism and liberal ideology or liberal cultural values are not the same. A distinction between liberalism as historical contingency and as recurring patterns of thought is also valid. The political map of liberalism is even more complicated. Some Dutch liberals consistently voted against the Liberal Party (VVD) and in favour of the Green Party. They should not be held responsible for the VVD 'liberal' reign in the Netherlands over the past years.

Our purpose is not just to prove critics wrong, however, but to see whether liberal ideals cope well with societal and technological changes. Is liberalism suited to the digital age, global economics, and climate change? Can liberalism survive in the era of post-truth? Can reason prevail over nostalgia and emotions? Is enlightenment not a fairy tale?

Liberalism never aspired to know the way to Utopia. Yet, its ambition was to offer a practical guide for solving conflicts, facilitating development, generating innovation, and securing freedom and social justice. We need to establish whether this ambition is still attainable in the Europe of the twenty-first century. Our historical knowledge suggests that no theories and practices are timeless and immune to political turbulence. Why would liberalism fare any better, especially with no major adjustments?

Ideology of Power

The word 'liberal' first took on a political meaning in Spain in the early nineteenth century and it has had many different incarnations since. Each of these emphasized different values and practices, but the key liberal principles are pretty straightforward and not contested by the vast majority of contemporary Europeans. Most Europeans believe in personal security, human independence, and individual liberty. They endorse democracy and the rule of law. They want the legal system to be impartial and democracy to be fair, tolerant, inclusive, restrained, and self-critical. True, liberals have always been accused of excessive individualism, rootlessness, permissiveness, material-ism, and cosmopolitanism, yet this normative criticism did not arrest their rising popularity in the 1980s and 1990s, nor can it explain their current falling-out with voters. The most frequent explanation of the liberals' current distress is the neo-liberal turn: classical liberalism has been captured and perverted by neo-liberalism, it is argued.

George Soros is probably the most prominent advocate of this position, but I gather from your earlier writings, Ralf, that you would side with his analysis. As Soros, himself a successful financial gambler, put it:

> The main enemy of the open society is no longer the communist but the capitalist threat...The doctrine of laissez-faire capitalism holds that the common good is best served by the uninhibited pursuit of self-interest. Unless it is tempered by the recognition of a common interest that ought to take precedence over particular interests, our present system—which, however imperfect, qualifies as an open society—is liable to break down...Too much competition and too little cooperation can cause intolerable inequities and instability.[6]

The question is: why was neo-liberalism able to prevail over other, more social, streams of liberalism? In the past, mainstream liberals like you, Ralf, believed in the provision of welfare and social justice. They emphasized the positive aspect of freedom (freedom to do something), and not just the negative one (freedom from something). They demanded public intervention on behalf of those deprived of liberty and dignity in various forms rather than on behalf of the fortunate few. What has happened to this egalitarian liberal stream? Has liberalism been hijacked by greedy bankers or was it an ideal breeding ground for self-indulgence?

Marxists believe in the latter; they have always thought that liberalism with a 'human face' is just a smokescreen for the capitalist system of exploitation.[7] They argue that the social market economy you were so fond of, Ralf, is an attempt to save capitalism from self-destruction. According to Marxists, the neo-liberal excesses have at last revealed the real nature of the system: 'the king is naked'.

This analysis is too crude and conspiratorial. In fact, even former Marxists within the counter-revolutionary movement such as Podemos or Syriza no longer cite their ideological masters. Yet, it is hard to deny that neo-liberal economics have generated winners and losers; the former represent a tiny minority and their prime source of income is rent from their vast assets. As Thomas Piketty convincingly argued:

Modern economic growth and the diffusion of knowledge have made it possible to avoid the Marxist apocalypse, but have not modified the deep structures of capital and inequality...When the rate of return on capital exceeds the rate of growth of output and income, as it did in the nineteenth century and seems quite likely to do again in the twenty-first, capitalism automatically generates arbitrary and unsustainable inequalities that radically undermines the meritocratic values on which democratic societies are based.[8]

The previous generation of liberals felt quite at ease with inequality; for them a more pressing social problem was poverty and dependence. They knew that economic competition would generate inequality, but they believed that competition would create enough prosperity to increase the welfare and personal security of all strata of society, including those at the bottom. Today we know that this was over-optimistic, to put it mildly.

It is fairly easy to blame neo-liberals for hijacking the liberal project, but I fear that this will not exonerate liberal politicians in the eyes of their voters. Communists in Eastern Europe also claimed that Marxism had been captured and perverted by the party apparatus led by such inadequate people as Brezhnev. Neither Marx nor Engels advocated invading Afghanistan, depriving workers of any genuine representation, tolerating rampant inequalities. Gorbachev tried to introduce communism with a 'human face'; he did not try to destroy the communist system. Yet, his efforts to reform communism proved futile if not counter-productive. People across Central and Eastern Europe had had enough of the regime systematically betraying its fundamental principles. Today, some elderly Marxists may have a feeling of déjà vu.

The second lesson from the Eastern European experience tells that revolutions or counter-revolutions are not just about economics, but also about regime change. As you argued, Ralf, the 1989 revolution was about democracy, security, Europe, borders, and culture, not just about bread and butter. People wanted to be governed by a different kind of politician. They resisted the ideology of power that purported to have 'correct' answers to all these important issues. I fear that the situation today is similar. Since 1989 liberalism has not just been a widely used map to guide individuals, governments, and societies; it has become the official governmental map dictated by the liberal elite in power across Europe. Put differently, liberalism has become a comprehensive ideology of power: a set of values, a way of governing, and a cultural ethos. Today, the insurgents across Europe rebel against the entire liberal system. They do not distinguish between good and bad (or accidental) liberals, between genuine and sham liberal ideals, between familiar or alien cultural patterns. They want to get rid of the entire liberal package. Different liberal politicians, from the centre-left and the centre-right, are being smeared. A vicious campaign is being forged not only against neo-liberal economics, but also against liberal democratic constitutionalism, against the liberal notion of open borders, against directives coming from Brussels, even against manifestations of the liberal culture. Under the counter-revolutionary assault is feminism, multiculturalism, abortion, gay rights, and environmentalism. Poland's minister of foreign affairs from the counter-revolutionary PiS, Witold Waszczykowski, went as far as to mock publicly 'a world made up of cyclists and vegetarians, who only use renewable energy and fight all forms of religion'.[9]

The analogy with 1989 has its limits, however. In 1989 people wanted to embrace the Western type of liberalism, which was then seemingly kinder and more successful than is the case now. Democratic and economic experiments were few and they were quickly abandoned. Imitation was the rule of the game if only because accession to the EU demanded adoption of 20,000 laws and regulations cooked up in Brussels. Today, it is not clear what the counter-revolutionaries want to build on the remnants of the liberal international order. There is no attractive alternative in sight to be followed. Policy prescriptions of the insurgents are patchy and they vary widely. Putin's Russia or Xi's China may well offer financial help to some of the counter-revolutionaries, but they do not offer a governance model that is sufficiently appealing and suitable for cloning. Nor are they able to define the notions of legitimacy, efficiency, and justice. In short, they lack the ideological power that liberalism possessed.

However, this ideological power has been a mixed blessing for liberalism. Liberalism is no longer an ideology of those oppressed by the state; it is an ideology of the state run by the mainstream centre-left and centre-right parties. Liberalism is not defending minorities against majorities; it is minorities—professional politicians, journalists, bankers, and jet-set experts—telling majorities what is best for them. By shifting ever more powers to non-majoritarian institutions, liberals have effectively deprived the electorate of a say on politics. By privatizing and deregulating the economic sector liberals have effectively prevented the electorate from changing the course of economic policies. Liberals have also spread, and some would say 'imposed', their atomistic model of society, their interpretation of history, their favourite films, even their dietary habits. It would be wrong to assume that all this was the function of commercial relations and the search for profits. From 1989 liberalism has been a comprehensive 'bible' on what is good or wrong in a society, not just a manual for making money. Liberalism defines a notion of what is rational and appropriate. Like all powerful ideologies liberalism is able to define the notion of normality. The counter-revolutionary politicians do not just oppose individual liberal policies, they defy the entire liberal logic. They try to introduce a new normal. They try to reject liberal truths.

Post-Truth

These days the favourite liberal term for scoffing at counter-revolutionary forces is post-truth. 'Populists' are accused of twisting facts, manipulating statistical data, and lying. They are being blamed for playing on voters' prejudices, sentiments, and emotions while ignoring evident truths and facts.

Liberals' critiques are justified; counter-revolutionary politicians are indeed masters in entertaining post-truths. However, liberals crying foul has two limitations. It is hard to see the nascent era of post-truth as the main reason for the liberals' electoral misfortunes, and liberals have made their own significant contribution to the spread of misinformation, sexed-up facts, political branding, and fake news. Tony Judt grasped well the atmosphere within liberal circles a few years ago: 'We all lie, they all lie, goes the reasoning. The question is: is he your liar or my liar?'[10]

Post-truth is not just about lying, which is as old as human communication. Nor is post-truth about dogmatism, self-confidence, and arrogance. Politicians, like theologians, tend to have 'the only correct view' on most things. Clearly, they cannot all be right. Post-truth is defined by the Oxford dictionaries as 'relating to or denoting circumstances in which objective facts are less influential in shaping public opinion than appeals to emotion and personal belief'.[11]

The word 'post-truth' can be traced back to as far as 1992, but I do not recall you ever using it, Ralf. This is probably because you disliked buzzwords, but also because Europe was somewhat different at the time of your major writings. In fact, documented usage of the term 'post-truth' increased dramatically only over the past two or three years; by 2,000 per cent in 2016 compared to 2015.[12] Yet, the causes of the problem are indeed two or three decades old and thus coincide with the triumphant liberal era. Some of the causes relate to the digital (technological) revolution, while others relate to the post-modern (cultural) revolution. The ever greater availability of statistical data, complexity of human transactions, plurality of opinions, and sophistication of communication channels are well-known implications of these revolutions. Liberals, unlike conservatives or communists, feel at ease within the new environment: they have always cherished pluralism, free speech, and free choice while refusing any simple truths and dogma. For most of them there is no one truth, but many truths, depending on the context and interpretation. Liberals have problems with those who claim a monopoly on objectivity and impartiality. For them the notion of what is just and fair can best be established through democratic bargaining along certain procedures, and not by reading the Bible or *Das Kapital*. The best science, in their view, emerges from questioning the established truths and orthodoxies. All this is fine for you and me, Ralf, but it paves the way to post-truth: if there is no one single truth, how do we know whether our truths are better than those of the political adversaries? Are not truths with a better spin and PR likely to prevail? Will not those with connections and money try to impose their own truths on all of us?

These may sound like abstract philosophical questions, but they have been addressed by political and economic entrepreneurs in a quite pragmatic and, at times, ruthless fashion. Over the past several years we have experienced a proliferation of institutions gathering statistical data and the rise of the 'facts industry'.[13] Such entrepreneurs are able to sell their 'scientific' results directly to the masses with the help of smartphones and laptops. On Facebook, Twitter, or WhatsApp everybody can be a provider of facts and truths, but the competition requires sophisticated marketing skills, extensive PR, and effective spin. Each provider of new 'evidence' has to distinguish her or his truths from those provided by others. More often than not it pays to be outrageous rather than just objective or 'truthful'. We now have sites generating 'fake' news and those trying to counter them with true truths, so-called fact-checking sites. Most of these adversarial sites claim to use 'scientific' evidence.

'Consumers' of many competing, and often contrasting, facts and truths are increasingly confused, distrustful, and biased. They tend to form like-minded clusters; they trust only facts that support their personal views or feelings. Technology reinforces that kind of partisanship. Facebook's algorithms are designed to crowd their newsfeeds with content similar to material they previously 'liked' or shared. Thanks to such a 'filter bubble', xenophobes are most likely to see racist items, and probably think that their views are popular if not legitimate.

Liberals who have controlled most of Europe's governments over the past two or three decades have done little to arrest this trend. What's worse, they have regularly exploited opportunities created by the communicative chaos, and sometimes even purposefully encouraged media decadence. 'Evidence-based' reasoning has notoriously been used and misused by liberals to justify governmental programmes and policies. Liberal politicians have relied heavily on PR agencies and spin doctors. Inconvenient facts are either removed from the political discourse or discredited by 'scientific' advisers on the governmental payroll. The most striking British examples concern the 'evidence' regarding the weapons of mass destruction in Iraq and the Brexit statistical scorecard foreseeing '£15bn tax rises, increase in fuel and alcohol duties and £15bn cuts to health, education and defence' if Britain leaves the EU.[14] In Italy the government employed numerous 'scientific' experts arguing that voting 'no' in the 2016 constitutional referendum would cause an immediate economic catastrophe, while in Poland the government effectively silenced environmentalists in order to protect its generous policy towards the mining industry. Similar examples abound in other countries. No wonder the counter-revolutionary politicians have adopted a similar tactic and often prove more skilful in generating cooked-up evidence supporting their own partisan, if not outrageous, positions. Predators feel at home in the jungle, don't they?

Not only liberal politicians, but also liberal intellectuals have made their contribution to the spread of post-truth. I don't have in mind those 'postmodern' social scientists insisting on personalized, relativized, subjective, and floating truths. I have in mind those intellectuals who intentionally present a one-sided picture of complex social and economic reality. Would you be able to explain, Ralf, why our liberal colleagues have articulated numerous theories of European integration and not a single theory of European disintegration? It is like studying peace without studying war; one may well prefer peace over war, but one cannot understand the former without comprehending the latter. Likewise, one cannot study democracy while ignoring autocracy. If one wants democracy to last, one needs to understand factors generating its opposite: autocracy. Yet, in European studies nobody ever attempted to talk about disintegration. Why was this so? I guess, some of us did not want to encourage the unwanted scenario, while others feared losing EU funds. Whatever the answer, we lack much-needed knowledge on how to arrest disintegration and resist the Eurosceptics' propaganda.

It would be foolish to accuse liberals of failing to censor fake news and halting the spread of new communication technologies, yet some criticism of their positions is certainly justified. Had liberals led by example and refrained from generating their own semi-truths, they would be in a stronger position to counter the wave of fake news and other forms of distorted realities propagated by the opposite camp. Had liberals constructed rather than dismantled institutions aimed at guarding the accuracy of news reporting and preventing the misuse of statistical data, it would be harder for political demagogues to influence the general public. With no reliable referees or trusted gatekeepers the producers of fake news and virtual truths can only prosper. Had liberals refrained from confusing ideological myths with facts, the counter-revolutionary forces would have found it hard to propagate their own legends. Whether a country can or cannot afford more generous social policy, for instance, is not just a function of statistical facts but also of political choices. Much depends on one's conception of good and justice, not just on one's statistical skills. Yet, those suggesting a minimum wage or a bonus for an additional child are branded by (neo)liberals as irresponsible populists. As Andrew Calcutt concludes in his analysis of post-truth: 'Instead of blaming populism for enacting what we set in motion, it would be better to acknowledge our own shameful part in it.'[15]

Lost in the Universe

In February 2017, Marine Le Pen told the cheering crowd in Lyon: 'The French have been dispossessed of their patriotism. They are suffering in silence from not being allowed to love their country.'[16] Such arguments are being echoed by counter-revolutionary forces across the entire continent. They point to two kinds of liberal failing. First, liberals are being blamed for embracing Europeanization and globalization. Second, they are being accused of ignoring or even bashing patriotic feelings of belonging to a given nation. Both criticisms appeal to citizens who feel lost in the global liberal universe with no sense of community and protection. Supporters of Le Pen, Orbán, Farage, or Kaczyński believe that only nation-states can stand for their economic, cultural, and political rights and offer them a better future. Our liberal friends rightly dismiss such thoughts as naive and dangerous, yet they fail to offer a convincing, let alone appealing, vision of a global liberal society. This may explain their current political troubles, at least to some extent.

One does not have to be a xenophobic nationalist to see the liberal conception of society as vague and abstract. A respected body of liberal thinkers including Michael Walzer, Michael Sandel, Philip Selznick, and Charles Taylor have pointed to this 'liberal myopia', but with the advent of neo-liberal canons their concerns have been ignored by the mainstream liberal parties and media.[17] Communitarian liberals pointed out that mainstream liberalism pays special attention to individuals rather than communities, and these individuals are seen as free, tangential, and private—accepting communal obligations only in order to minimize their risks. Liberals have usually little time for family or religious bonds, national or ethnic history, corporate or class association. Some of these groups are even seen as a source of evil. Religious fundamentalism or ethnic fanaticism are not only illiberal and irrational, they have been responsible for violence and oppression. At best, liberals talk with empathy about individuals forming a civil society, that is, a community of citizens freely engaged in political, economic, and social forms of non-governmental and non-profit work.[18] Yet, even these kinds of bond are viewed with suspicion by some liberals. Members of racist associations can also be seen as a kind of civil society, they argue. The very fact of belonging to a community does not represent a virtue for many liberals; what counts is endorsement of liberal values in theory and practice. As Stephen Holmes forcefully argued: 'There would be no terrorism or nationalistic border wars without selfless devotion to social groupings ... Those who have homosexuals shot in the name of the Islamic revolution ... cannot be accused of antisocial individualism or base self-interest.'[19] Besides, granting some communities special favours is seen as wrong by liberals. Why should Christians be treated differently from atheists or Muslims? Why should persons of a certain race or ethnic background have privileges?

So far so good, but does our liberal vision sufficiently account for people's fears and passions, collective bonds and traditions, trust, love and bigotries? Real life is not just about commonly agreed procedures, rational institutions, and abstract fairness. People are born in families with certain views and connections, they grow up in certain places with history and culture, they work and socialize with people who are often emotional and biased. Liberals are suspicious of all these communal and often primordial links, which explains why they are often seen as detached from the 'real people'. Most persons have national pride, religious beliefs, and political prejudices. They feel 'at home' with like-minded and like-looking people, they trust those whom they know, they entertain peculiar habits, sentiments, and myths. Liberal calls to rely on evidence, reason, and experts fall on the deaf ears of people attached to places, communities, and particularistic (often old-fashioned or narrow-minded) ideas. Liberals may well know how to defend individuals from bad laws, religious orthodoxy, or ethnic hatred, but they have little to say on how to create harmony, solidarity, and communal spirit, which are needed for any serious collective endeavours. It is not even certain that a notion of a good society and justice can be spelled out and agreed upon without a reference to a certain group of people, living in a certain territory and sharing a certain historical, cultural, and moral perspective. It is hard to claim that these arguments merely represent populist demagoguery.

Nationalism is the number one enemy of liberals, not only because it has led to plentiful wars and pogroms.[20] Nationalism discriminates against ethnic minorities and migrants, which is illiberal. Nationalism is about myths rather than reason; it is about primordial rather than civic bonds; it is about a forcible assimilation to a single group rather than about individual freedom. It is hard to disagree with such assertions. However, liberals cannot but admit that freedoms are chiefly guaranteed by states, or to be more precise, nation-states. Democracy, as you, Ralf, often reminded us, has also functioned well only in nation-states. And thus, getting rid of nations may well destroy the very fundamentals of democracy, the rule of law, and individual freedom. Most virtues of the liberal society have been possible thanks to nation-states, and not to any abstract political constructions.

For liberals it is particularly hard to cope with demands of national (and territorial) independence within multi-ethnic states. Liberals found ethnic wars in the former Soviet Union and the Balkans repulsive, and exotic. In the recent years, the cases of Scotland and Catalonia have also left liberals confused and divided. I am completing this letter at the time Europe's eyes are focused on the conflict over the Catalonian declaration of independence from Spain. The outcome of this conflict will have profound implications for the liberal project, but European liberals seem unable to go beyond vague calls for dialogue, democracy, and constitutional order.

Because the liberal conception of society is universal rather than linked to a certain place or nation it is only natural for liberals to embrace transnational politics and economics. Liberal ideals were behind the creation of the United Nations and the European Communities. Free trade, multilateralism, and cultural exchanges are among the prime means of advancing the liberal project. In short, liberals belong to the 'party of globalization' and not to the 'party of territoriality', to use Charles Maier's expression.[21] The question is: who will secure the liberal order in a world of fuzzy borders and cascading interdependence? The only transnational public authority of any meaning, the European Union, is now in the process of decomposition. International organizations such as the United Nations or the World Bank can hardly shield individuals from predatory economic and political behaviour. Does any genuine liberal still believe that the American empire is indeed an agent of freedom around the world?

Will a Russian or German 'empire' do any better in their respective European neighbourhoods?

In the Europe of the 1960s and 1970s much of the liberal discourse was about the welfare state and the idea that mutual responsibility, the recognition of interdependence, and a sense of community were the means to support individual development. This discourse has gradually evaporated since 1989. Neo-liberals (under the influence of Reaganomics) have introduced a false dichotomy between liberalism and communitarianism. The former was to be all about individuals: 'there is no such thing as society', famously declared Margaret Thatcher. As a result, the liberal project has left individuals lost in the maze of powerful transnational markets and deficient transnational institutions. Increasingly citizens find themselves isolated and deprived of public protection be it in the field of economics, law, or administration. We undermined national borders without creating effective transnational public authorities. The counter-revolutionaries are probably naive to think that a return to nation-states will solve any major problems, but I wonder whether liberal freedoms can still be protected in a Europe we liberals have created. I also wonder whether liberalism can effectively be defended without a collective will, solidarity, and hope bordering on myth. We failed to create a European civil society and a European public authority able to push forward the liberal project. No wonder more and more European citizens are abandoning us and are instead endorsing outdated but familiar policies of national glory, moral community, and walls separating one group from another.

What Good am I?

Liberalism has been scorned and proclaimed dead a few times in history, most vividly in the nineteenth century and then in the interwar period of the twentieth century. Yet, it always bounced back and may well do so again in the future. In fact, liberals are still holding on to power in several European states and we should not assume that the days of liberalism are numbered.

This does not mean that its current critics will soon disperse and liberalism will again be 'the only game in town' across Europe. I don't want to sound pessimistic, Ralf, but I fear that liberal ideals will be under assault for some time and will bounce back only after a long and probably traumatic period of history. Let's hope it will not be as bad as in the 1930s and 1940s, but we cannot be sure. To bounce back, liberals would need to rethink their vision of democracy, capitalism, and European integration. Preaching abstract liberal principles and bashing anti-liberal opponents will not do. To bounce back, liberals need also to change their leaders because those who compromised, or even betrayed, the liberal project cannot be entrusted with renewing it. Above all, liberals ought to admit their errors, not just to regain credibility among the voters, but also to understand where improvements ought to be made.

In 1989 Bob Dylan wrote a song that could become the liberal motto for the next few years:

> What good am I if I know and don't do,
> If I see and don't say, if I look right through you,
> If I turn a deaf ear to the thunderin' sky,
> What good am I?
> …
> What good am I if I say foolish things,
> And I laugh in the face of what sorrow brings,
> And I just turn my back while you silently die,
> What good am I?[22]

I have tried to convey to you, Ralf, what liberals have ignored or done incorrectly. I have failed to do this as concisely and poetically as Bob Dylan, but three terms or, if you wish, values have come to the fore repeatedly: equality, community, and truth. They are now on the banners of counter-revolutionary politicians. Liberals should try to regain these terms for their own project.

There is no chance for equality to be taken seriously without abandoning neo-liberal economics. This is not just a question of economic theory; there are vested interests behind neo-liberal economics, and genuine liberals need the courage to stand up against them. Yet, their struggle against neo-liberalism will not succeed as long as there is no plausible alternative vision of capitalism in sight. (I will write more about the neo-liberal notion of capitalism later in this letter.)

Liberals cannot just think and talk about individuals and their liberty. They should start seriously thinking and talking about communitarian bonds, social responsibility, and their potential for securing liberal freedoms. As Philip Selznick argued many years ago, 'The thin theory of community espoused by many liberals is not enough … we need a stronger idea of community, one that will justify the commitments and sacrifices we ask of ourselves, and of one another, in the name of a common good.'[23] I am not sure whether a kinder version of nationalism is a viable option, a 'liberal nationalism' as Stefan Auer put it.[24] Most probably a new, and somewhat utopian, vision of a communitarian republic ought to be envisaged with the help of digital means of public deliberation. Whatever the option taken, leaving communal issues to counter-revolutionary forces would marginalize liberals and expose Europe to all negative manifestations of communitarianism: national belligerency, ethnic hatred, and religious fundamentalism in particular.

Last, but not least, liberals ought to embrace truth. By this I do not only mean refraining from lying or confusing facts with interpretations and opinions. Nor do I want to advocate any ideological truths. As Michael Freeden explained, 'If liberals do subscribe to a notion of truth, that truth is experimental and subject to changing historical and spatial understandings.'[25] By embracing truth I mean genuine efforts to comprehend present-day Europe and the concerns of its citizens. Agonizing about the latest opinion polls, flashing comfortable statistics, and spinning political images go in the opposite direction.

By embracing truth, I also mean searching for novel liberal solutions to key challenges of the twenty-first century such as peace, sustainable development, climate change, migration, and equality. Before we rush to any action we need to understand the issue we are trying to address and our (in)capacity to improve things. This is not easy in the heat of the current political battle, but we need to find a proper balance between denouncing and explaining. We cannot just engage in finger-pointing at our opponents who prevent us from setting things right; we also need to look in the mirror and comprehend our own failings. The explainers tend to justify wrong-doing: is not globalization responsible for populism? Yet, the denouncers do nothing to explain: look how destructive populists are!

One cannot understand the world without any normative compass, which obviously requires us to make certain judgements. Yet, judgements cannot be applied only to our opponents, but must also appertain to ourselves. We need repeatedly to ask: what good am I? Do I live up to my liberal standards? Only then will we be able to teach by example, which Hannah Arendt conceived as an ideal link between truth and politics. As she put it in her famous 1967 essay: 'teaching by example is, indeed, the only form of "persuasion" that philosophical truth is capable of without perversion or distortion.'[26]

3

DEMOCRATIC MALAISE

You, Ralf, had no doubt that the liberal type of democracy is superior to the 'egalitarian' one. Democracy, you argued, is a form of government, not a 'steam bath of popular feelings'. Government by the people you called a 'democratic illusion' paving the way for usurpers and monopolies. 'We the people' can rise against an abhorrent regime of exploitation and suppression, but 'we the people' cannot govern, in your view.[1] The current counter-revolutionary movement is trying to prove you wrong and popular support is increasingly on their side.

The reasons why ordinary citizens are today disillusioned with the liberal type of democracy are many and they are legitimate. To start with, the application of your liberal principles went much too far: democracy has become an art in institutional engineering with little space for citizens' participation. Elections are organized, but they fail to generate genuine policy changes, while key decisions are being taken by unelected bodies such as central banks, constitutional courts, and the European Commission.

The institutional pillars of liberal democracy are also in crisis. Political parties have become 'cadre' and 'cartel' parties with few members and no loyal electorate; the executives treat citizens as consumers, subject to refined instruments of public opinion testing; the hegemonic mass media have replaced parliaments as the key forum for political debate. Mimicking democracy has become easy in this situation and this generates public outrage.

With the arrival and subsequent domination of neo-liberal economics a more fundamental question has also been posed: can democracy still control the markets? And if not, can politicians implement any of their electoral pledges regarding such fundamental issues as pensions, investments, or even health care?

Our liberal friends would share some of these concerns, but they would argue that the counter-revolutionary politicians will not bring power back to the people, as they claim to. They will probably establish a kind of *anocracy*: an inherently unstable and ineffective government regime displaying an 'incoherent mix of democratic and autocratic traits and practices'.[2] I fear that this will indeed be the case. Getting rid of the liberal democratic order is one thing; constructing a genuine, but also well-functioning participatory or egalitarian democracy is another. Yet, we cannot understand the current counter-revolution without acknowledging the flaws in the liberal project. And we cannot dismiss efforts to renew democracy simply because they are being pushed forward by political adversaries. In the history of democracy, the most significant advances resulted from heated and at times violent political struggles. The rulers, however enlightened, are seldom eager to grant more rights to the ruled.

Was liberal democracy ill-conceived or just badly executed? Probably both. Most crucially it failed to adjust to rapid changes in the fields of economics, communication, and culture. Stakeholders' communities correspond to national borders less and less. The internet has created new opportunities for citizens to monitor politicians, and for politicians to monitor citizens. Modernization and migration generated cascading fragmentation, polarization, and instability making it difficult to mediate public preferences. Liberal democracy offered few plausible solutions for coping with these challenges, and it has also become hostage to vested interests operating in the shadow of formal democratic laws. No wonder some citizens gave up on democracy while others began to rebel.

Dysfunctional Representation

The counter-revolutionary politicians pretend to speak on behalf of people who no longer feel represented in the system of government.

Why is their claim credible? Because the pillars of political representation are in tatters, namely parties, parliaments, elections, and the media. Erosion of these basic pillars of representation has clearly intensified over the last decades and coincided with the triumphant liberal era. A quick look at cross-European statistical data shows that over the last two decades we have experienced record low levels of electoral turnout, of party membership, and of public trust in parliaments.[3] In the same period we could observe record high levels of electoral volatility, progressively benefiting counter-revolutionary politicians.

We do not need to study speeches of counter-revolutionary politicians to see a sweeping crisis of political representation and its basic institutional pillars. As an Irish professor, Peter Mair, put it boldly: 'Although the parties themselves remain, they have become so disconnected from the wider society, and pursue a form of competition that is so lacking in meaning, that they no longer seem capable of sustaining democracy in its present form.'[4]

Parties are anything but dead. They may have few members, most of whom are relatively old,[5] but they have more power and resources than ever. The problem is that today in Europe party funds come chiefly from the state rather than membership fees, private donors, and affiliated organizations. The power of parties also comes from state regulations rather than strong roots within respective electorates. Parties no longer act as a bridge between the state and society; they have become part of the state machine, detached from the electorate. Parties are basically relying on state-regulated channels of communication; they use state facilities in order to staff and support their own undermanned organization; and they reward their supporters and activists with the state's privileges and resources. This explains why parties are still alive and kicking but this does not make them representative. The gap between ordinary citizens and the party elite is growing wider and it is being filled by the new kids on the block with counter-revolutionary banners.

Parliaments are said to be the key sites of political representation: this is where laws are being made and governments are being scrutinized. In reality, most laws are being prepared in ministries usually headed by party leaders with parliaments rubber-stamping their decisions, often with little discussion. The scrutinizing of politicians is mainly taking place in the media, increasingly online. Even special parliamentary committees established to air major misconduct of officials are run as public relations exercises and hardly ever lead to disciplinary actions against party leaders.

Gone are the times when parliaments pretended to resemble a marketplace of ideas with great doses of inspiring eloquence; today, parliaments are voting machines disciplined by party whips. Debates are still taking place in parliaments and they are often aired on TV channels, but they bear little resemblance to the ideal of deliberative democracy. MPs follow the party line and throw insults at each other, sometimes even leading to violent brawls. Examples of compromise and mediation between the ruling parliamentary majority and minority are scarce these days even in countries such as the Netherlands that used to pride themselves on a consociational political culture. If one adds to that successive scandals involving parliamentarians, such as the 2009 expenses scandal in the mother of all parliaments, Westminster, then it is easy to understand why this pillar of representation is increasingly wobbly.

At present, citizens place parliaments at the bottom of the list of institutions that deserve their confidence or esteem. According to the 2016 Eurobarometer only 28 per cent of Europeans tend to trust their national parliament. Spanish citizens' net trust decreased by 67 per cent in a short period between 2008 and 2010, and that of Irish citizens declined by 65.7 per cent. Decline of trust in parliaments, albeit less drastic, has also been observed in economically prosperous countries such as Germany.

Given the deficiencies of contemporary parties and parliaments it is not surprising that elections are no longer being seen as a political game changer. In fact, rallies of counter-revolutionary movements such as Podemos are full of banners saying: 'vote without voice'.

Elections are being organized and celebrated, but they do not make the voters feel listened to and represented. Elections change parties in power, but unless counter-revolutionaries triumph, elections hardly lead to major changes in economic, cultural, or migration policies. Voters can punish ruling politicians, but they are unable to bring them closer to their homes, workplaces, and daily concerns. Voters can only watch competing politicians at a distance, with few opportunities for dialogue of any significance. Elections increasingly resemble heavily mediated carnivals. Spin, image, and deception prevail over substantive arguments and historical record. And since we are living in the era of post-truth, competing electoral contenders can get away with ordinary lies and smears.

This brings us to the fourth key pillar of democracy: the media. The 1989 liberal revolutionaries in Eastern Europe campaigned for free and independent media. However, they soon discovered that in democracy the media are also being manipulated not just by local politicians, but also by corporate interests. Silvio Berlusconi's political PR machine proved more skilful than any communist propaganda and it found many followers across the continent. Not only television, but also the quality European press has become increasingly opinionated, partisan, and sensational. Democratic politics is for them a kind of entertainment, generating income. Politicians with no social roots and straightforward views need to adjust to media requirements. No wonder they often talk like reality show contestants on the screen. Some of them even take part in such television shows as *Strictly Come Dancing* or *Big Brother*.

The internet has offered channels of communication free from editorial censorship, but these channels have often been skilfully exploited by those indulging in hate speech rather than in the promotion of democracy. The internet has helped citizens to monitor politicians and to connect with each other. However, access to the internet is unequal, both in terms of provision and consumption. The private data of citizens are being used and misused by internet providers and security agents. Some information (however false) is being spread, while other information (however accurate) is being silenced. According to Buzz-Feed News, spreading deceitful information on Facebook and Twitter has become the daily bread and butter of politics in many democratic states.[6] In sum, the internet has been a mixed blessing for representative democracy, at least so far.

Liberal Oligarchy

It is unfair to blame liberals for all the problems of democratic representation. Social modernization and the spread of new technologies such as the internet have made our societies more pluralistic and fragmented. This in turn has made it difficult for parties to mediate, aggregate, and then represent adequately all the competing preferences of their traditional voters. Long-standing ideologies and institutional arrangements became obsolete and there was little time and consensus to make democracy work in a novel way. Yet, some of the counter-revolutionary politicians proved more eager to engage in democratic experimentation than the established ones. They highlighted contestation and direct participation as the most important democratic pillars. For instance, the Spanish Podemos and the Italian Five Star Movement have utilized the internet for permanent consultations between their leaders and supporters. In Madrid, where a coalition backed by Podemos governs, the mayor has earmarked €60million of spending as a 'participatory budget', to be decided through online polling, with proposals submitted via local assemblies. Liberals were quick to ridicule these participatory experiments. Their preferred type of democracy was increasingly seen as elitist or even oligarchic.

Democracy was never about a simple will of the majority of the day in a parliament. The majority is constrained by numerous constitutional provisions; the power in democracy is divided between the legislature, the executive, and the judiciary. Moreover, constitutions guard the rights of minorities against the hegemonic aspirations of majorities. Liberals always campaigned for more rights for different kind of minorities. Migrants, gays, racial or ethnic groups, children, and disabled people have progressively been defended by law or even granted preferential treatment. This made some segments of the local majority uneasy. One does not need to be a xenophobe to fear the competition of well-skilled migrants ready to work for lower wages, for instance.

Shifting power and resources to institutions not directly elected has also frustrated the majorities. Constitutional courts, central banks, and numerous regulatory agencies were progressively granted powers to act against the will of parliaments. This was not a liberal plot to dispose of the sovereign people, as often claimed by the counter-revolutionaries. Constitutional courts are part of the checks-and-balances and their role is to ensure that politicians do not interpret the basic law in a partisan manner, defy it, or ignore it. Central banks are to ensure that politicians do not manipulate monetary policy for their political ends. Regulatory agencies are said to possess highly specialized expertise lacking among parliamentarians. They are also able to adopt a longer time perspective than the usual electoral cycle. As Giandomenico Majone argued:

> credibility, rather than the legitimate use of coercion is now the most valuable resource of policy-makers. Unfortunately, it is quite difficult for democratic politicians to credibly commit themselves to a long-term strategy: because a legislature cannot bind another legislature, and a government coalition cannot tie the hands of another coalition, public policies are always vulnerable to reneging and thus lack long-term credibility. Hence, the delegation of policy-making powers to [non-majoritarian] independent institutions is a means whereby governments can credibly commit themselves to strategies that would not be credible in the absence of such delegation.[7]

This reasoning especially applies to such fields as health, environmental protection, and pensions, where short-termism is irresponsible.

The problem is that issues tackled by non-majoritarian institutions are not just technical; more often than not they are political. Politicians tend to make excessive promises, especially before elections, but it is wrong to assume that voters blindly trust all these 'unrealistic' promises and therefore they need 'independent' and 'objective' judges, bankers, regulators, and other kinds of expert to step in and 'correct' the sovereign. In democracy people and their elected representatives should have the right to shape the notion of collective interest, and not unelected experts. For instance, experts argue that rising pensions will increase inflationary pressures and will also put a greater burden on the future generation of employees. Nevertheless, it is doubtful whether experts or even judges (let alone bankers) should be in a position to decide the retirement age or the scale of benefits.

Non-majoritarian institutions pride themselves on being objective and non-partisan, but this is frequently not the case. Judges and experts have their political friends and ideological prejudices. What is objective knowledge can be debatable in some cases. And as Alec Stone Sweet rightly observed: 'When the court annuls a bill on rights grounds, it substitutes its own reading of rights, and its own policy goals, for those of the parliamentary majority.'[8] The same can be said about central banks or regulatory agencies.

As always, much depends on the issue, context, and proportions. Most citizens would probably prefer it if such issues as food safety or air traffic be handled by experts rather than politicians, especially on a day-to-day basis. The problem is that the proliferation of non-majoritarian institutions with ever greater powers has gone too far over recent years, causing public anxiety. Liberals ruling Europe have been accused by counter-revolutionary politicians of governing without an electoral mandate, using courts, central banks, and experts to bypass or paralyse parliaments. Even in the United Kingdom, judges were called 'enemies of the people' by pro-Brexit tabloids.[9]

These accusations gained credibility in countries where liberals lost elections to counter-revolutionary politicians. In Hungary, Greece, and Poland defeated liberals relied on the power of appointed constitutional judges or central bankers to boycott or annul decisions or laws adopted by the new governments. The counter-revolutionary politicians in turn were quick to neutralize these non-majoritarian institutions and staff them with their own political allies. In an act of anti-liberal and anti-European defiance, Poland's governing party PiS has ignored the Constitutional Court's rulings and accused it of playing politics. It has then adopted laws making it difficult for the Court to function properly. Laws ought to be made in the parliament representing the majority of Poland's electorate, PiS argued, and not by unelected judges trying to preserve the old liberal order. Liberals organized a series of mass demonstrations in defence of the Constitutional Court, but polls have not shown a reversal of public support in favour of liberal politicians.

People feel insufficiently represented not only because of formal institutions and laws; informal rules and institutions are just as important. Counter-revolutionary politicians have been particularly effective in convincing the general public that liberal democracies are being run by an informal network of politicians, lobbyists, bankers, and media moguls. The evidence for the existence and power of these networks is sketchy if only because they are never transparent, institutionalized, and accountable. We know that Rupert Murdoch's empire had close relations with numerous British politicians, but the nature of these relations is still mysterious despite such official proceedings as the Leveson Inquiry.[10] In Italy the fusion between the media, business, and politics has not been confined to Silvio Berlusconi. Most Italian newspapers and television broadcasters are linked to a network of partisan industrialists and politicians. The case of Carlo de Benedetti, a well-known Italian industrialist, is a case in point. De Benedetti has led an anti-Berlusconi media campaign using his own liberal newspaper La Repubblica. When Berlusconi was ousted from power, La Repubblica helped the centre-left party of PM Renzi (and de Benedetti himself) to combat the counter-revolutionary critique of Beppe Grillo and his Five Star Movement.

The counter-revolutionaries claim that liberal informal networks operate in a mode of dirty togetherness by exchanging favours, fencing off competition, and promoting partisan regulatory standards. The loyalty of these networks is based on common history and interests rather than common ethical, professional, or political values. They are by nature elitists and discriminate against the ordinary people and those who pretend to speak for them. Liberal networks not only promote friendly politicians, but also propagate convenient ideological canons and expedient statistics. They ridicule alternative ideas and silence inconvenient truths. Sadly, there is some truth in counter-revolutionary claims that democracy is progressively oligarchic: a relatively small elite is trying to govern according to its own vision of the world with little effort made to listen to the electorate.

The masses (read: the ordinary voters) have been portrayed by liberals as naive and irrational if not drunk or insane. Asked to explain the electoral victory of anti-revolutionary PiS in 2015 elections, Adam Michnik, an editor of the liberal daily *Gazeta Wyborcza*, said: 'Sometimes a beautiful woman loses her mind and goes to bed with a bastard.'[11] Supporters of counter-revolutionary politicians such as Le Pen, Farage, or Wilders have been branded xenophobes and racists. Brexit campaigners were accused of 'mad slur[s]'.[12] Of course, we may think that the electorate has made wrong choices, and democracy is not merely about 'the voice of the people'. Yet, it is hard to imagine a democracy that does not respect electoral outcomes, and liberals are not likely to get voters back on their side by insulting them and calling them foolish, incapable, and naive. Defeated liberals should ask themselves the question 'why have the citizens voted for the counter-revolutionary forces and not for us?' Liberal oligarchy as practiced after 1989 is certainly one of the reasons and ought to be repudiated by liberals themselves. Unless liberals are able to make citizens feel that their voices really count, the counter-revolutionary forces will push for a pure electoral democracy with no respect for minority rights, checks-and-balances, and the division of power principle.

External Veto Players

The democratic problems discussed so far are domestic by their nature and can probably be remedied by purposeful political pressure and institutional engineering. The ballot box can remove arrogant politicians from office and the powers of non-majoritarian institutions can be curbed by parliaments or popular votes adjusting the existing constitutions. It is trickier to deal with challenges and problems that are by their nature transnational. Over the past two or three decades we have come to realize that progressive globalization and European-ization have generated a new constellation of territory, authority, and rights.[13] This could not but affect democracy.

Democracy is chiefly confined to the territory of nation-states, but are these nation-states still in charge of what takes place within their borders? If not, how can democracy secure the rights of its citizens? How can it be receptive to electoral demands? There is not a day that passes by without politicians blaming global markets, EU regulations, German obstinacy, or transnational human traffickers for the lack of electoral responsiveness. Democracies seem no longer sovereign. Electoral choices seem not to matter much in the world of cascading interdependence.

National politicians continue to promise many things ahead of elections, but they are increasingly unable to deliver on these prom-ises because of mounting external constraints. The electorate keeps removing from power politicians who fail to keep their promises, but this does not lead to any meaningful policy changes. Powerful transnational forces tie politicians' hands and render the sovereign will of the people illusory.

We could debate for a long time whether states and their respective *demoi* were ever fully sovereign within their borders. Some of them, particularly large and rich ones, were always more sovereign than the others, which led some scholars to call the principle of sovereignty a kind of organized hypocrisy.[14] Globalization and regionalization are not entirely new phenomena either and it is hard to blame the winners of the 1989 revolution for all their negative consequences. Yet, liberals have enthusiastically embraced globalization and European integration with profound implications for the democratic politics of nation-states.

Most crucially, markets are now largely freed from democratic controls. At the same time, they impose their own restraints on democracies. If the movement of capital across borders can hardly be monitored, let alone curbed or taxed, democracy becomes powerless. If public spending cannot be maintained even by such opportunistic measures as inflation or public debt then most electoral commitments are void by definition. If European markets are being flooded by cheap goods produced by underpaid and unprotected workers in Asia then it is hard for European governments to introduce a statutory minimum wage for their own local employees. If factories threaten to move abroad when faced with trade union pressure or increased taxes then democratic governments have very little room to manoeuvre indeed.

To be responsive democracy must have the means to influence, if not control, transnational markets. It also needs to operate in a space corresponding to the scale of the markets. In other words, there ought to be a matching transnational public authority for regulating transnational markets. This is what European integration was all about, wasn't it?

The EU was supposed to help Europeans cope with transnational pressures. By territorially enlarging and institutionally enforcing the system of governance, the EU was intended to empower European citizens. Unfortunately, this proved not to happen. The EU has consistently been more responsive to the demands of business lobbyists than those of ordinary citizens. It turned out to be 'a Trojan horse' reinforcing the continued dominance of the markets over democracy.[15] Already in 2001 a wide coalition of groups dismissing the EU as undemocratic and as an agent of globalization clashed with police on the occasion of the EU summit in Gothenburg, devastating a large part of the old city. After 2008 the EU has also become hostage to the most powerful creditor states, Germany in particular. Demonstrators in numerous Greek cities burned EU flags and carried banners portraying Angela Merkel as Adolf Hitler.

The EU's failure to create a democratic public authority on a transnational basis may have vindicated your own scepticism, Ralf. As you once wrote: 'apart from nation-states, we shall never find appropriate institutions for democracy'.[16] Democracy as we know it emerged in a process of state and nation formation which is difficult to replicate in different settings. For instance, the system of democratic representation can hardly work properly without a clearly defined *demos*, and we do not have such a *demos* above nation-states.[17] At best we have a collection of *demoi* which do not form a coherent whole.[18]

Moreover, democracy does not only require the creation of some democratic institutions such as parliaments, elections, or constitutions; it also requires territorial borders that correspond and coincide with systemic functional boundaries, and that are in line with the consolidated socio-political hierarchies within the corresponding populations.[19] Only nation-states were able to achieve the latter, and without it democratic institutions may remain empty shells, offering a misguided feeling of democratic normalcy, but hardly any genuine legitimacy.

If you are right, Ralf, I no longer see any future for democracy. It is naive to believe that nation-states can turn back the clock of history and regain control over transnational flows of capital, goods, labour, refugees, ideologies, and communication. Does anybody believe that after Brexit Westminster will get a handle on global capitalism? I even wonder whether Westminster will get a handle on global migratory flows. Of course, this is not a zero-sum game. Theresa May or Boris Johnson will argue that regaining some control over trans-border migration, communication, and trade is a bonus for Westminster. The question is: at what price? Their effort may well generate profound conflicts without adequate gains in mitigating the negative effects of globalization and regionalization. The Russian and Chinese autocrats have more means and determination to control their borders, but they are also unable to stop capital flows and internet penetration. Besides, transnational trade and communication are not just a threat for democracy; they can also represent a great asset. Much depends on whether they work for the benefit of citizens and under their supervision. Do they empower or enchain citizens?

How Does One Empower Citizens?

The post-1989 liberal elite assumed that governance is a kind of enlightened administration on behalf of an ignorant public. They failed to get rid of policies and people that proved inefficient, sometimes even corrupt. They compromised their liberal principles when pressed by partisan lobbying. Democracy stopped performing its legitimizing and representative functions as a consequence. It not only lost its purpose, but also its sex appeal. It has become 'oligarchy, formally legitimized by general elections'.[20] Today, we bear witness to a powerful counter-revolution which aims at dismantling liberal democracy and replacing it with a new puzzling, and perhaps frightening, form.

This is the irony of history, as the 1989 revolution was said to have ended any competition to liberal democracy. However, it was not expected that democracy left without any serious competition would degenerate beyond recognition, becoming chiefly a procedural exercise deprived of political substance, historical memory, and ethical purpose. It became a ceremonial cover-up for very complex global operations that are largely unaccountable, if not secret. This was skilfully exploited by counter-revolutionary politicians.

Democracy has always been contested by both the rulers and the ruled and we can probably talk about a permanent crisis of democracy. We may not have any democratic advances without these crises. In this sense the counter-revolutionary quest for a more inclusive form of democracy has some virtues. The current crisis of democracy stems partly from the erosion of the main pillars of parliamentary representation. However, it also stems from the erosion of the key democratic units: nation-states. Globalization and interdependence have not only eroded nation-states' ability (and desire) to control the flow of goods, money, services, and people; they have also transformed European *demoi*. They are increasingly pluralistic, multicultural, and complex. Political loyalties and cultural identities are increasingly transnational. The digital revolution has offered new ways of public deliberation and participation. As administrative borders, military frontiers, cultural traits, and market transaction networks increasingly diverge we are being invited, if not forced, to reconsider the relationship between *demos, telos,* and *kratos.*[21]

Democracy has never been static, but adaptable in response to material and ideological pressures. On the eve of the twentieth century many parliamentary governments were still dependent on their local monarchs, elections were hardly free, and electoral rights were severely restricted. In France and Belgium women were allowed to vote only after the Second World War. There is no reason to assume that democracy cannot be adjusted once again, even though we do not know yet the direction of this change. At present, more and more decisions affecting respective national electorates are being taken by various supranational bodies or by global economic, regulatory, or even judicial networks. This has prompted calls for a new type of cosmopolitan democracy.[22] Such calls are tempting, but difficult to implement. Constructing democracy at a European level seemed modest in comparison with democracy at a global level, and yet the results were disappointing.

That said, democracy will not be saved by reverting to nation-states; it can only survive, or even thrive, by adjusting to the new interdependent world. The EU failed because it never fully embraced democracy, not because democracy beyond nation-states is impossible. There is no reason to believe that people will ever give up their struggle for political and economic rights. And if so, they will look for new ways of bringing transnational actors under some form of public scrutiny.

Democracy does not need to be chiefly about national representation; it can also be about transnational contestation and direct participation, possibly with the help of the internet. Democracy does not need to be confined only to states. Cities and regions are already viable democratic units; a struggle for democracy is also being forged within multinational firms and international organizations. The point is not to create a global or regional super-state with state-like democratic institutions. The point is to make the dense web of global networks more transparent, accountable, and responsive to people's ancient quest for freedom and equality.

This proposition may now seem complex and impractical, but the history of democracy shows that there are no simple and quick solutions for empowering the people. A good example is recent referenda. Referenda are said to let citizens decide the most crucial issues, but in reality they resemble a festival of political folly dominated by rough and artificial arguments. This is especially the case when referenda concern complex and highly politicized issues rather than local practical issues related to citizens' daily experiences. (In Switzerland most referenda fall into the latter category.) The question—'Should the United Kingdom remain a member of the European Union or leave the European Union?'—involves a different kind of knowledge, deliberation, and choice than the question 'Should car traffic in the medieval centre of our city be restricted?' A simple Yes and No in the former case has more profound and largely unpredictable consequences than in the latter case. Moreover, a referendum leaves no space for mediation and compromise between conflicting parties. The losing minority, however large, can hardly be accommodated by the wining majority, however small. In each referendum the winning majority takes all, the minority loses all. No wonder that some democracy scholars fear that such an 'outright zero-sum mechanism of decision making' may well lead to a 'majority tyranny'.[23]

The situation is even more problematic when only a fraction of the European electorate is able to cast a vote on matters concerning Europe as a whole. Recently, we had four such referenda: a referendum asking Greek citizens to support a deal negotiated by their government with European creditors, a referendum asking Dutch citizens whether they approved the Association Agreement between the EU and Ukraine, a referendum asking British citizens whether they wanted to stay in or leave the EU, and a referendum in Hungary on whether to accept mandatory EU quotas for relocating migrants. In all these cases the winning, and often narrow, majority within a single country was able to damage a policy enjoying overwhelming support in numerous other European countries. Is this not a clear example of a minority tyranny?

An institutional device which creates conflicts, rewards demagoguery, hype, and spin, as well as generating accidental rather than fair and effective outcomes can hardly be seen as democratic and empowering the people. We need to look for more efficient and intelligent ways of empowering people in the ever more interconnected regional and global setting. Of course, this is easier said than done, but we need to keep trying.

4

SOCIALISM FOR THE RICH

European economies used to provide growth and social justice, but we have seen little of either in recent years. Before the 2008 financial crash it was still possible to argue that Europe is on its way to becoming a global economic superpower that made many people look at it with admiration, desire, and jealousy. As Jeremy Rifkin put it in his 2004 book *The European Dream*:

> Europe has achieved newfound dominance not by single-mindedly driving up stock prices, expanding working hours, and pressing every household into a double-wage-earner conundrum. Instead, the New Europe relies on market networks that place cooperation above competition; promotes a new sense of citizenship that extols the well-being of the whole person and the community rather than the dominant individual; and recognizes the necessity of deep play and leisure to create a better, more productive, and healthier workforce.[1]

However, within a few short years this enthusiastic assessment has been replaced by the rhetoric of pessimism and doom. In 2013 François Heisbourg declared the 'end of the European dream', Anthony Giddens called Europe a 'turbulent continent', and George Soros talked about Europe's 'tragedy'.[2]

Most of this gloom has been caused by the profound crisis of the European single currency, but the Euro was only one pillar of the liberal economic mythology that was debunked by the financial crash. Other pillars of this mythology stipulated that markets are rational, inequality stimulates efficiency, banks are responsible players, and privatization and marketization of the public sector will make it thrive.

This was neither intended nor expected. The 1989 revolution was said to have banished communist ghosts once and for all. Privatization and deregulation were supposed to free citizens from misguided central planning and an oppressive state. The free market was said to empower citizens and help them develop entrepreneurial skills. Social policy was to become real and not just declaratory. In your *Reflections on the Revolution in Europe* you indeed praised free-marketers from Central and Eastern Europe—Leszek Balcerowicz and Vaclav Klaus—and you urged your Polish friend to be patient because some pain was needed before Poland would construct a *soziale Marktwirtschaft* (Social Market Economy) on the model designed and implemented in your native Germany by Ludwig Erhard and Alfred Müller-Armack. Balcerowicz and Klaus have indeed created a free market in their countries, but they neglected and, some would say, actively erased the social aspects of it.

The liberal or, as it has usually been called, the neo-liberal economic revolution may have been forged more speedily and perhaps more brutally in Central and Eastern Europe, but it was not invented there. Balcerowicz and Klaus were simply imitating Ronald Reagan and Margaret Thatcher who in the 1980s initiated massive deregulation, privatization, tax cuts for the rich, outsourcing, and competition in public services. These policies were soon adopted by Europe's socialist leaders, most notably by Tony Blair and his New Labour. The International Monetary Fund, the World Bank, the European Commission, and the World Trade Organization followed suit. Neo-liberalism has become a new dominant economic paradigm, with no competition in sight.

The Social Market Economy has not been renounced, if only because the European public, perhaps unlike the American one, has a strong attachment to public health, education, and transport. State aid to those in need is widely accepted in Europe. All this requires taxation and redistribution according to commonly agreed rules. However, the new liberal rhetoric in Europe argued that socialism can go hand in hand with capitalism, that the private sector can perform public functions, sometimes better than the state itself, and that marketization enhances growth and efficiency benefiting not just the rich, but also the poor. This was the essence of the 'third way' programme embraced by most left-wing parties. Christian democrats and conservative liberals may have had less time for socialism, but they believed that capitalism should be compassionate to some degree, and they have not pushed the free market agenda as much as Reagan and Thatcher did. The popular continental slogan has always been that Europe should embrace the Stockholm consensus rather than the Washington consensus, the former combining productivity with generous welfare.

Today, we cannot but conclude that the Social Market Economy is in tatters across Southern Europe and seriously diluted even in such proficient states as Germany and Sweden. Inequality is surging within and across countries, with no U-turn in sight. Public money is chiefly used to help large multinational banks, but not to help small investors getting off the ground or researchers inventing new technologies. Tax havens are tolerated, while state pensions are being cut.[3] Governments seem determined to clamp down on unemployment benefits, but not on executive directors' huge bonuses. Zero-hour contracts are spreading, and trade unions are portrayed as harmful relics of the past.

Karl Marx must be laughing in his grave. The marriage of markets with the state has generated socialism for the rich and capitalism for the poor. The Social Market Economy is now an empty phrase in most European countries. The anti-liberal forces are promising to restore some sense of social justice, but the damage seems beyond repair. It is difficult to forge any meaningful redistribution with national budgets heavily in debt, and hardly any economic growth.[4]

From Crisis to Crisis

European officials used to say that Europe comes out stronger from each crisis. This time, however, we are faced with multiple crises, each reinforcing another, with no plausible solution in sight. The list of crises is long and ever growing. We have a banking crisis, a debt crisis, a currency crisis, a growth crisis, a crisis of inequality, a crisis of cohesion, a crisis of work, and, above all, a crisis of imagination, which means that we have no idea how to get Europe's economies out of the current mess. Critics of neo-liberal follies are recommending a reversal back to Keynesian economics based on a cocktail of financial and monetary policies—chiefly low interest rates and government investment in infrastructure. But can the prescriptions effective on the eve of the twentieth century cure the patient on the eve of the twenty-first century? The scale of financial services, globalization, and climate change was of a different order in the age of John Maynard Keynes, and they required different solutions. For instance, Keynesianism stimulates consumer demand and economic growth, but both lead to environmental destruction. Moreover, Keynesianism requires the existence of strong public authorities. Yet, globalization and neo-liberal reforms have vastly reduced nation-states' regulatory capacities without creating effective transnational public institutions to fill the gap. The impotence of the EU to contain the monetary and fiscal crisis within its space bears witness to the latter. Greek transfers of its 'sovereign' rights to a consortium of creditors bear witness to the former.

The chronology, intensity, geography, and nature of each of the crises differ, but they all seem overwhelming. Let's start with the crisis of the banking system, often seen as the prime pillar of capitalism. The collapse and subsequent nationalization of the Northern Rock Bank by the British government in 2007–8 was the first sign of this crisis. Numerous banks across the continent have found themselves insolvent since then and have sought support from their respective governments. Monte dei Paschi di Siena, rescued by the Italian government in late 2016, has survived adverse economic conditions since 1472. It is the oldest bank in the world and therefore its current predicament is very telling. Equally telling are rumours regarding the insolvency of such contemporary giants as Deutsche Bank or Société Générale. Their fall would bring the entire European banking system to its knees; a dire prospect indeed. There is no point in entertaining the worst case scenarios, but given that trillions of Euros and pounds were spent propping up the banks over the last decade you will not be surprised to learn, Ralf, that Europe's electorate is rather unhappy and is looking for new politicians to clean up the banks. After all, most of the money to the banks in the form of direct financial help, insurance, or cheap funding came from taxpayers' purses. Helping banks meant less money for social policy and an ever-growing public debt, which leads me to another serious crisis.

The public debts of several European states have sky-rocketed in recent years. Some states (Greece, Portugal, Ireland, Spain, and Cyprus) were unable to repay or refinance their government debt or to bail out over-indebted banks under their national supervision without the assistance of third parties such as other Eurozone countries, the European Central Bank (ECB), or the International Monetary Fund (IMF). Italy was able to service its debt, representing 132 per cent of the country's GDP (in 2015), but it required an immense sacrifice on the part of ordinary Italians. Even Germany's government debt/GDP ratio is over 70 per cent, up more than 30 per cent since the early 1990s. The reasons behind the rising debts vary from country to country and so do the countries' ability to service them. That said, accumulated public debts across the continent are confronting governments with difficult budgetary choices.

There is now abundant evidence to conclude that austerity policies are hindering the economic recovery; yet, throwing money 'out of the helicopter' as recommended by some economic specialists will not necessarily generate growth.[5] Europe has seen little growth since the early 1990s despite numerous economic stimuli, some of them responsible for the current level of debts. To be more specific, the GDP growth rate in the Euro area averaged 0.37 per cent from 1995 until 2016, reaching an all-time high of 1.30 per cent in the second quarter of 1997 and a record low of −3 per cent in the first quarter of 2009.[6] Clearly some factors other than fiscal policy are behind Europe's sluggish growth.

A handsome growth rate does not prevent the rise of a counter-revolution, however, as was illustrated by the Polish case. Poland's GDP grew over 20 per cent in the last decade and yet in 2015 the electorate opted for a government running on an anti-liberal ticket, promising a major change of economic policy. The key factors for the electorate's seemingly irrational behaviour was the crisis of work and inequality. Poland's unemployment rate of circa 8 per cent compares well with Spain's unemployment rate of circa 19 per cent. However, Poland is a champion in precarious, that is, zero-hour contracts that give employees little or no job security and social benefits.[7] Poland is also a champion in earnings disparities; the 10 per cent best-paid employees earned at least twice as much as the 10 per cent lowest-paid in Sweden, and nearly five times as much in Poland.[8] In 2015 the electorate clearly voted on the basis of their daily economic experience, ignoring the rosy growth statistics spread by the liberal elite.

Needless to say, problems are of a different order in Greece, which has experienced a fall in GDP of more than 20 per cent over the last decade. Unemployment in Greece is circa 25 per cent (with youth unemployment reaching 50 per cent) and the government debt represents 181 per cent of its GDP. The Greek case shows that inequality within states goes hand in hand with inequality among the states of Europe. This may not be surprising, but discrepancies have grown rapidly since the outbreak of the 2008 financial crisis. Several years ago unemployment in Spain was at a similar level to that in Germany, for instance. Today, Spain has five times more unemployed people than Germany. Greece and Cyprus are no longer sovereign states, but semi-protectorates run by a consortium of creditor states represented by the IMF and the Eurogroup.

This brings us to the crisis of the European single currency, the Euro. The Euro was meant to boost the economic fortunes of its members, but it achieved the opposite; stagnation within the Eurozone is greater than outside it. The Euro was also meant to provide a greater convergence among its members, but again it achieved the opposite; it exacerbated the gaps and conflicts between the surplus and deficit countries, the importers and exporters, and the North and South. Hardly anybody believes that Greece will ever repay its debts despite three consecutive bailouts, and yet both Greece and its creditors stick to this unworkable arrangement because they fear that ejection of Greece from the Eurozone may spark a domino effect destroying not only the Euro and Greece, but also the entire EU. (Greece's current debt in absolute terms is several billion less than six years ago, but due to the economic collapse the debt ratio nevertheless rose from 113 per cent to 181 per cent of GDP.)

The public in both creditor and debtor states is unhappy with the current situation, and liberals are getting the blame.[9] The public in the indebted countries resents the creditors' diktat which forces them to endure painful cuts to social spending in particular. Yet, the public in the creditor countries is not enjoying the situation either. Bailout arrangements are expensive and provide no prospect of debts being repaid. They blame the debtor states for living beyond their means and for cooking the books. However, debtor countries point out that the dysfunctional single currency arrangement was not invented by them, but by France and Germany. They also point out that Germany has actually benefited from the crisis and failed to offer its fair contribution to compensate the losers of the common market and currency.

As always, the real picture is more complex than simple stereotypes. Unlike Italy or Greece, Spain and Ireland had modest debt levels prior to the crisis and therefore cannot be accused of living beyond their means; their problem was a property bubble, which points at market deficiency or at the real estate developers' greed. Inequality is caused by many different factors; it is simplistic to think that inequality exists because some people have a Protestant work ethic while others indulge in leisure. The Euro may have been poorly constructed, but it functioned well before the financial storm, which originated in New York, not in Frankfurt or Brussels. Greek banks may well have been run poorly, but they were not responsible for the sovereign debt burden of Greece becoming unsustainable and a tempting target for speculators. Generous social spending has not prevented Sweden or

Finland from being champions in work productivity. Romania's low social spending has not visibly increased the country's productivity. Economists try to explain different parts of the puzzle, but if you ask me what is the prime factor behind the series of crises currently facing Europe, one stands above all. Its name is economic neo-liberalism.

Neo-liberal Revolution

You, Ralf, would certainly be surprised to see neo-liberalism as a synonym of liberal politics on the eve of the twenty-first century. For liberals like you, neo-liberalism was just a small fundamentalist sect within the large liberal family. You even compared Friedrich Hayek, the best-known proponent of neo-liberalism, to Karl Marx: 'Like Marx, Hayek knows all the answers...[he] is an all-or-nothing theorist...which is dangerous if not disastrous in the world of real political conflicts.'[10] How one can be a dogmatic, fundamentalist liberal is a puzzle to me. Is not liberalism about freedom to choose, which by itself demands tolerance and flexibility?

Yet, it was Hayek, not open-minded social liberals like you, Ralf, who conquered the hearts of Ronald Reagan and Margaret Thatcher. They used the power of their office to push through a dramatic, and you would perhaps say doctrinaire, reordering of not just the economic system, but capitalist society as such. Today, most mainstream politicians, journalists, and bankers are insisting that there is no alternative to the dogma of free market, free trade, free choice, free competition, and free community. Anything else is called irrational, irresponsible, and futile. Neo-liberals were thus able to define the notion of normality, which is the perfect definition of the ideological dominance that survived the financial meltdown with no meaningful alternatives in sight.

The repertoire of neo-liberal politics is well known: the privatization or marketization of public services such as energy, water, trains, health, education, roads, and prisons; removing or reducing state regulation of such vital economic sectors as trade, industrial competition, financial services, communication, energy, health, and environment; reduction of taxes, especially for big business, and toleration of tax loopholes; decreased social support and stringent means testing for groups still eligible for public help such as the unemployed, disabled, homeless, or single parents.

Money was allowed to buy nearly everything during the neo-liberal era, including a dinner for Ferrari clients on the medieval bridge in Florence (Ponte Vecchio). Money has also become a prerequisite of 'respectable' non-governmental work and social protest. Even the anti-corporate Occupy Wall Street has taken donations from business leaders, while prominent NGOs have formed formal partnerships with multinational corporations.[11] Oxfam has teamed with Nokia and Marks & Spencer, and Greenpeace with Unilever and Coca-Cola.

The private sector has vastly expanded at the expense of the public sector; profits were usually privatized while the state was left with the risks. The distinction between the public and private spheres has been effectively blurred and public money is now spent on actors and causes with dubious public credentials. According to the National Audit Office (NAO) in the United Kingdom, around half of what is spent by the public sector on goods and services now goes to private contractors, some of them helping the state to reduce welfare spending or boost deregulation of trade and financial services.

Although Friedrich Hayek in his acclaimed book published in 1944 asserted that 'socialism means slavery' and that government intervention, by crushing individualism, could lead to totalitarian control, the politics of his disciples proved more nuanced or, if you wish, hypocritical.[12] Contemporary neo-liberals are indeed alarmed when the state helps pensioners and the unemployed, but happy when the state helps failing banks and inefficient car factories. They dislike state support for public schools and hospitals, but like state support for private schools and hospitals. They constantly demand state intervention to advance the neo-liberal economic model and complain when the state is too weak to comply with their demands. In other words, the neo-liberal condemnation of state interference in markets and fostering of redistribution is quite selective. What neo-liberals propose is well grasped by Owen Jones: 'Socialism for the rich: sink-or-swim capitalism—and food banks—for the poor...While the financial elite could depend on the state to swoop to their rescue, those who suffered because of their greed felt the chill winds of laissez-faire.'[13]

The 'natural' outcomes of such policies are cascading inequalities in wealth and opportunities, within and across European states. At present, inequalities are a matter of concern even among CEOs gathering in Davos, and Thomas Piketty's 704-page-long book containing ninety-four graphs is a bestseller.[14] For many years, however, inequalities have been tolerated, rationalized, and sometimes even encouraged by neo-liberals. To this one should add injustices of class, gender, and ethnicity, economic exploitation at home and abroad, corruption and money laundering—all representing the neo-liberal legacy. Whether they have been generated by default or design is a matter of discussion which is not likely to be settled soon.

By now we also know the selective meaning of freedom advocated by neo-liberal promoters. As George Monbiot put it concisely in his critique of neo-liberalism: 'Freedom from trade unions and collective bargaining means the freedom to suppress wages. Freedom from regulation means the freedom to poison rivers, endanger workers, charge iniquitous rates of interest and design exotic financial instruments. Freedom from tax means freedom from the distribution of wealth that lifts people out of poverty.'[15] Can such definitions of freedom be called liberal?

Even before the 2008 financial meltdown neo-liberal economics had been accused by Susan Strange of running a casino capitalism.[16] After the 2008 breakdown neo-liberal economics was blamed by Naomi Klein for creating a disaster capitalism.[17] Whatever the label attached to this kind of economics we know that it has cost ordinary taxpayers trillions of Euros, dollars, or pounds invested in failed banks and other malfunctioning businesses. The unemployed, the underpaid, and the uninsured show the real price of these policies together with bankrupt cities, regions, and even states, failed schools, impoverished hospitals, overcrowded prisons, broken highways, and collapsing bridges.[18]

Naomi Klein was right in saying that the appetite for easy, short-term profits offered by purely speculative investment has turned the stock, currency, and real estate markets into crisis-creation machines. The 2008 breakdown was not the result of incompetence or misman-agement. It was the logical consequence of a system glorifying rough competition, demonizing public intervention, and justifying wide-spread inequalities. We do not even need the 2008 breakdown to manifest the neo-liberal fallacy. As Joseph Stiglitz pointed out, eco-nomic growth has actually slowed down 'as the rules of the game were rewritten to advance the interests of banks and corporations—the rich and powerful—at the expense of everyone else'.[19] Even the IMF admitted that lower net inequality is robustly correlated with faster and more durable growth.[20] So much for the efficiency and wisdom of neo-liberal free markets.

Buying Time

Why has neo-liberalism not been abandoned in the aftermath of the 2008 crisis? Why have liberals allowed the counter-revolutionary movements to lead the angry and impoverished voters against the neo-liberal folly? Those on the left such as Syriza or Podemos have always been against globalization and big business, but those on the right, such as Front National, Fidesz, and PiS have jumped on the train of public rage with no particular economic legacy or expertise. To see Marine Le Pen or Jarosław Kaczyński as prominent defenders of social justice and advocates of economic renewal is a paradox of history.

Marxists would tell us that people with money can always manipu-late politics, and when we see major parties accepting money from some of the biggest tax evaders we're tempted to believe them.[21] Those with money were also financing propaganda machines glorify-ing neo-liberal virtues and concealing their deficiencies. It is not easy to trace the mechanism of neo-liberal economics though.

As Monbiot argues: 'Anonymities and confusions mesh with the namelessness and placelessness of modern capitalism, the franchise model which ensures that workers do not know for whom they toil; the companies registered through a network of offshore secrecy regimes so complex that even the police cannot discover the beneficial owners; the tax arrangements that bamboozle governments; the financial products no one understands.'[22] The wealthy also used carrots and sticks. The latter were particularly directed against those who offered resistance to neo-liberal policies, trade unions most notably.

The problem with the Marxist explanation is that neo-liberal policies are currently benefiting only a tiny part of the 'capitalist class': the well-off middle classes of entrepreneurs are shrinking, and those truly profiting are now the famous 1 per cent—or even 0.1 per cent.[23] Why did the majority of entrepreneurs put up with this, let alone ordinary citizens? The answer is probably that they were left with no political representation. Europe's social democrats embraced neo-liberalism and preferred to join forces with their historical arch-enemies on the right of the political spectrum than with the new counter-revolutionary forces. Greek PASOK formed a government with New Democracy to fence off competition from Syriza. Italian Partito Democratico collaborated with right-wing friends of Silvio Berlusconi to combat the rise of the Five Star Movement. Spanish Socialists could not imagine an alliance with Podemos. This has something to do with diametrically different political cultures within the established socialist parties and the left-leaning new kids on the block. But it has also, if not chiefly, to do with the historical trajectories of European social democrats.

The last important socialist leader trying to defy the business barons was François Mitterrand. He won the 1981 presidential elections in France promising a 'complete rupture' with capitalism and tried to stick to his promise by nationalizing some industries, increasing state spending, and extending the rights of French employees. He soon had to deal with a revolt by financial markets, weakening of the franc, businesses moving abroad, and angry voters. Mitterrand quickly reversed his policies and other socialist leaders in Europe took note.

Tony Blair did not try to refute neo-liberalism, but rather tried to give it a human touch, with rather mixed results. Even in Scandinavian countries, social democrats reconciled themselves with corporate demands to curb labour rights and welfare spending.

The EU has also failed to curb the neo-liberal excesses. Formally, the EU is not in charge of taxation and its competence in the field of social policy is symbolic. Moreover, the EU progressively embraced the neo-liberal agenda of deregulation, marketization, and privatization. Let's not forget that there are now more than 30,000 lobbyists registered in Brussels trying to influence the decisions of the European Commission in charge of the single market.[24] The European Council is also dominated by eminent representatives of the neo-liberal establishment. When, in the middle of the Euro crisis, the Greek socialist Prime Minister, George Papandreou, announced his intention to hold a referendum on the acceptance of the neo-liberal terms of a Eurozone bailout, he was forced to step down under the pressure of his fellow European leaders. Alexis Tsipras was also told by European leaders to 'put up and shut up' a few years later, even after the majority of Greeks opposed the creditors' diktat in a referendum.

These last examples suggest that politicians trying to run against the neo-liberal order stand little chance. As we noticed in the previous chapter, democracy has probably lost control over markets. Yet, the counter-revolutionary surge suggests that the business community may pay a high price for sticking to neo-liberal recipes. The counter-revolutionaries may have few insights into businesses and markets, but they may complicate their life tremendously, sometimes even through sheer incompetence. The business community needs stability not chaos; it needs workable institutions, the rule of law, and political consensus of some sort. The counter-revolution puts all this at risk.

The question remains, however: what are the plausible liberal alternatives to neo-liberalism? In October 2016 the newly elected leader of the British Conservative Party admitted that 'the roots of the revolution run deep. Because it wasn't the wealthy who made the biggest sacrifices after the financial crash, but ordinary, working class families.'[25]

She therefore pledged an overhaul of corporate governance, including appointing consumers and employee representatives to British board-rooms. She also promised to end the 'anything goes' culture in executive pay. While these proposals ought to be applauded, one wonders whether they can achieve Mrs May's objective of securing 'fairness and opportunity' for ordinary working-class families. Besides, given the resistance of the business community, one should not assume that these proposals will ever be implemented.[26]

On the left of the political spectrum, abandoning austerity policies has been advocated as the main means to protect social benefits and reduce inequality. For instance, the head of the Socialist group in the European Parliament, Gianni Pittella, entered the race to become the next European Parliament President, by promising to run on an anti-austerity agenda. Moreover, he called for a major investment plan to reduce unemployment among young people, 'the very tragedy of Europe' as he put it.[27] Again, these are noble objectives, but they are not likely to change the way capitalism works at the moment. Besides, to be implemented these proposals would need to receive the backing of the creditor states, Germany in particular.

Politicians have a natural tendency to muddle through and buy time. They hope that problems will simply go away with time after cosmetic adjustments, and if some problems are to explode it is prudent to apply delaying tactics, they reason. Pressed by capricious opinion polls the time horizon of politicians is, after all, shorter than even the electoral cycle. However, Wolfgang Streeck has rightly argued that tactics of buying time are not working any longer. Infla-tion, public debt, private debt, illusions of growth, all these formerly successful means of appeasing citizens and markets seem exhausted.[28] Europe is running out of time.

One Billion Bitcoin Question

Perhaps we have no option but to conclude that the neo-liberal policies have damaged capitalism beyond repair. A return to the Social

Market Economy seems unrealistic at present. Governments are happy to address some of the immediate needs of the poor, but unwilling and unable to change policies fundamentally and jump into the unknown. Bold reforms are contentious while timid ones are useless. Hardship is spread unevenly within and across countries, and even those who are on the losing side do not see a viable alternative. For most employees, poor pay is better than no pay, zero-hour contracts preferable to no contracts, and unsafe work better than no work. States with unemployment of over 25 per cent have different priorities from states with unemployment below 5 per cent. The interests of users and providers of financial services are not necessarily as compatible as is often claimed. I am not even talking about the divergent perspectives of those at the top and at the bottom of the social ladder. How to make capitalism work for ordinary European citizens is a one billion bitcoin question. The point is not only to devise a new system, but also to get it through the existing structures of power and money.

When it was obvious that communism was damaged beyond repair, sceptical Poles used to respond to Gorbachev's attempts to reform it by saying, 'you can make a fish soup out of the aquarium, but you cannot do it the other way around'. By then, it meant the total rejection of communism. I fear that the liberals are not even prepared for the total rejection of neo-liberal economics. Are they prepared for a total rejection of capitalism? If not, what is their plan B? Can capitalism be reinvented in a fundamental manner? Is post-capitalism a catchword or a viable option?[29] I do not have an answer to these questions, and I fear that the counter-revolutionary politicians are not even asking such questions.

Successful alternatives to neo-liberalism would have to be comprehensive and not just deal with one aspect of economic policy such as taxation or banking regulation. They would have to envisage a new compromise between the winners and losers from transnational market competition because the system in which the winner takes all is not compatible with human dignity and democracy. They would have to restore a new balance between the public and private domains. The public sphere does not need to be identified only with the state; some regions, cities, and European bodies have already proved capable administrators of public issues. However, it is now evident that sound education, health, social welfare, culture, defence, and policing cannot be provided solely by the private sector following free market principles. In fact, the free market can hardly function without strong public authorities able to legislate, enforce, and arbitrate fair rules of market competition. Democracy would also need to be reinvented because the current model of territorial representation is not suited to handling trans-border economics. Europe would also need a new model of integration that recognizes local conditions and offers flexible, decentralized methods of governance based on meaningful incentives.

Even our brightest public intellectuals such as Wolfgang Streeck or Thomas Piketty are unable to give a satisfactory answer to our one billion bitcoin question. The winner will probably be announced several years from now, which explains why the award is in bitcoins rather than Euros. After all, the Euro may no longer be in circulation at the time of the awards ceremony.

5

GEOPOLITICS OF FEAR

You may ask me, Ralf, why the anti-establishment politicians and parties have gathered remarkable support only now. The evidence so far is fickle, but my guess is that it is mainly about insecurity. Never before over the last three decades have so many citizens feared for their jobs, health insurance, and pensions (and those of their children). They usually lay the blame for this on the liberal policy of globalization. For many people, going to their favourite restaurants or holiday beaches seems to be a risky business after a series of terrorist attacks. The liberal policy of open borders and humanitarian foreign intervention is often seen as a source of terrorism. Some people have even started to fear another war in Europe. Yet, liberals promised a peaceful and integrated Europe.

Perhaps liberals failed to strike the right balance between freedom and insecurity. Perhaps they simply didn't live up to their liberal vision of the world. Perhaps the liberal vision of the world was utopian. Whatever the answer, the world has become a pretty unsafe place during their reign. Insecurity manifests itself in different fields; it is as much about perception as about reality; different people in different places feel insecure in different ways. It is the scale and intensity of this feeling that seems unprecedented in the last generation or two.

When people feel insecure, the time is ripe for a counter-revolution. No wonder the anti-liberal politicians exploit this public anxiety. Fear is a great mobilizing factor; when threats are imminent we demand immediate action and we are ready for a jump into the unknown. Yet, fear is not just caused by a well-known predator such as the Soviet Union before 1989. As Zygmunt Bauman explained in his book on fear, 'Fear is the name we give to our uncertainty: to our ignorance of the threat and of what is to be done—what can and what can't be—to stop it in its tracks—or to fight it back if stopping it is beyond our power.'[1] Yet, fear in contemporary Europe is real and not just manufactured by anti-liberal forces.

You may rightly point out that in the past insecurity has made people rally behind the established parties. In the 1960s and 1970s the crisis of the structures of political intermediation in Western Europe already stirred up anti-establishment revolts, but the majority of the electorate had little appetite for supporting politicians raising street barricades, let alone violence. This time it seems to be different. This is partly because insecurity seems closer to home, overwhelming, and multi-dimensional, and partly because the disappearance of the Soviet threat undermined international cohesion and a common sense of purpose. And it is increasingly evident that the establishment is unable to put the variety of diffused security threats under control. The counter-revolutionary politicians do not build street barricades; they present themselves as the only force able to reinstate a sense of security. As Marine Le Pen declared: 'France and the French are no longer safe. It is my duty to tell you so.'[2] And she added on another occasion: 'The war against the scourge of fundamentalism hasn't started, it must now be declared. That is the deep wish of the French, and I will put all my energy so that they are finally heard and the necessary fight is finally undertaken.'[3]

As always, local circumstances define priorities. In France and Belgium terrorism is now the major preoccupation; in Latvia and Estonia people fear Russia chiefly; and in Greece and Portugal people worry most about their jobs. Left-wing counter-revolutionary politicians emphasize economic insecurity, while right-wing ones emphasize insecurity on the streets. Yet, in all countries across Europe there is a sense that threats to personal lives are mounting while governments fail to address them convincingly.

Terrorism and economic hardship make people insecure in a direct, tangible way. No wonder that these are the security topics most exploited by counter-revolutionary politicians. International insecurity is something vague as long as there is no actual war, yet it can hardly be ignored by citizens and politicians. Dutch public opinion had little interest in the geopolitical brinkmanship in Ukraine before a plane full of tourists was shot down by Donbas separatists on its way from Amsterdam to Kuala Lumpur. The terrorism of so-called ISIS on Europe's streets is related to the geopolitical brinkmanship in the Middle East. Brinkmanship between Donald Trump and Kim Jong-un of North Korea may well lead to a nuclear war with grave implications for ordinary Europeans. As I will argue later, the economic hardship in Portugal and Greece is also linked to geopolitics albeit in a different manner. Various types of security are fused more than ever; this is what the popular buzzword—hybrid warfare—implies. Let's reflect on insecurity related to the tricky contemporary geopolitics before considering economic or even cultural insecurity.

Geopolitics used to be Europe's nightmare; manipulation, aggressions, and territorial conquests driven by national ambitions and ideological myths produced unspeakable human misery, especially between 1850 and 1878 and 1914 and 1945. The 1989 revolution seemed to put the ghosts of history to sleep. Ideological rivalry between communism and the 'free world' had ended with the victory of the latter. Europe's nation-states, East and West, decided to integrate further. The geopolitical map was transformed 'by telephone and check book rather than blood and iron'.[4] War in Europe was declared inconceivable with the fall of the Berlin Wall.

This rosy story proved too good to be true and la géopolitique de grand papa has returned with a vengeance. Today, Europe's small and weak states are again bullied by large states and large states are trying to balance each other. Key institutional pillars of the liberal order—the UN, the EU, the WTO, and NATO—are being questioned and undermined. Integration and multilateralism are subsequently in tatters. Europe's neighbourhood is again violent, impoverished, and autocratic, with security implications for the core of the continent. With the return of the old Hobbesian pattern citizens feel confused and increasingly insecure. They want to know who is responsible for the sorry state of affairs. Why are Russia and Turkey no longer Europe's allies? Why did Europe stand by when the Arab Spring began to falter? Is German power a threat or a blessing for the continent? Will Europe be able to maintain peace? There are no obvious answers to such fundamental questions and hence the anxiety, if not revolt, on the part of the population. Counter-revolutionary politicians are at the helm of this revolt.

Explosive Neighbourhood

When communism collapsed, the major preoccupation of Europe's politicians was to prevent instability in its immediate neighbourhood with a possible spillover to the core of the continent. The violent disintegration of Yugoslavia manifested the scale of the challenge. European armies found themselves impotent on the battleground in Bosnia; European border guards proved unable to cope with the tide of refugees fleeing violence; European politicians struggled to find a common diplomatic ground. This traumatic experience was not to be repeated and the answer of Europe was twofold: EU enlargement to Central and Eastern Europe and the European Defence and Security Policy. The latter has never been a great success, but the former has become Europe's famous trademark.

Robert Kagan has cynically observed that Europeans are unable properly to address security threats because they seem to 'live in a self-contained world of laws and rules and transnational negotiation and cooperation'.[5] Yet, the European failure to master a genuine common security and defence seems more grounded in practical rather than ideological causes. Consensus on security issues has always been difficult to reach among European states, and it did not make much sense to send soldiers to possible death on the basis of vague political declarations reflecting the lowest common denominator. This lack of consensus emerged from different geographic locations and military capabilities, and not just different ethical perceptions of war and peace. Poles worry chiefly about Ukraine and

Russia, Italians about Albania and Libya. States with a sizeable army, such as France and Great Britain, do not want their policies to be shaped by states with tiny armies such as Belgium or by those with no appetite for military combat such as Germany. And there was always a consensus that collective European defence should be handled by a genuine military alliance such as NATO with Americans firmly on board. Small EU peace-keeping operations have multiplied in recent years, reaching different and often remote places such as East Timor, Congo, Sudan, Afghanistan, Iraq, Lebanon, Bosnia, and Georgia. However, none of this amounted to a genuine common European security policy that would be able to address instability in the neighbourhood. For this a different strategy was conceived: a policy of EU enlargement.

EU enlargement was formally about adopting some 20,000 EU laws by the candidate states rather than about proper security measures. Yet, enlargement represented skilful power politics pacifying the external environment. In its essence enlargement was about asserting the EU's political and economic control over the unstable and impoverished eastern part of the continent through a forceful use of political and economic conditionality. True, the post-communist countries were not 'conquered' but invited to join the EU. Yet, the candidates were not in a position to negotiate the EU's demands. These referred not only to trade and industrial competition, but also to democracy, minority rights, and settling territorial disputes. Central and Eastern European states were eager to comply with Europe's strict conditions because at the end of the accession process they were offered access to the EU's decision-making process and economic resources. They were seduced by Western Europe's liberal discourse on democracy and economics. They wanted to escape their autocratic history and join the club of wealthy, secure, and free Europeans.

Enlargement policy transformed ten potential 'flash points' into relatively prosperous and stable EU member states. Yet, this success came at a price. Enlargement not only complicated the decision-making system within the EU, it also changed the European balance of power in Germany's favour. Enlargement has also represented a huge import of different security and economic preoccupations and of different legal and institutional cultures. Migration has also increased with enlargement. Already the 2004 referenda on the EU constitution in France and the Netherlands were largely about Polish plumbers and tulip pickers; the end result was highly disappointing for Europe's establishment.

Enlargement policy was subsequently put on hold and replaced by the EU Neighbourhood Policy. Europe's proclaimed aims remained the same: creation of 'a zone of prosperity and a friendly neighbourhood'.[6] Yet, the prospect of EU membership was no longer there for the neighbours. This changed their motivation dramatically. Moreover, the scale of challenges Europe faced in Egypt, Libya, Moldova, and Ukraine was arguably greater than was the case in Lithuania, Poland, or Hungary. Ukraine's citizens have repeatedly manifested their willingness to join the prosperous part of Europe, but the crony economics, inefficient administration, ethnic disputes, and Russian interventions have prevented them from achieving their aims. In North Africa and the Middle East, a mixture of colonial legacy, religious fundamentalism, and economic backwardness have frustrated the quest for democracy and closer ties with Europe.

One can assume that any EU policy would face numerous obstacles in such a complex neighbourhood, but security policy is not a zero-sum game. The relevant question is: has Europe developed a sound policy towards unstable neighbours after ditching the enlargement project? My answer is that the new policy towards neighbours was either naive or merely rhetorical. How else can one explain abandoning Libya after a forceful removal of Kaddafi's regime? A responsible security policy, let alone a humanitarian one, would not allow such a mess in Libya. Was there nothing Europe could do to help nascent democracy in Tunisia? When I visited Tunis a few days before the first terrorist attack in 2015 European officials were only interested in deterring potential Tunisian migrants from crossing the Mediterranean. Can Ukraine ever become a stable state without Europe's helping hand? President Poroshenko is being offered red carpets, lavish dinners, and numerous photo opportunities in European capitals, but very little results from his visits, photos, and dinners. The EU still refuses to give Ukraine significant economic aid or invest seriously in Ukrainian civil society institutions.[7] It is no exaggeration to say that George Soros has done more in Ukraine than the entire EU.

A decade after the launch of the Neighbourhood Policy, experts concluded that the policy is 'in tatters'. The aim was to 'encircle the EU by a ring of prosperous, stable and friendly countries', but instead the core of Europe 'finds itself in a neighbourhood characterized by conflict, counter-revolution and resurgent extremism'.[8] Instead of the envisaged 'ring of friends', Europe is encircled by 'a veritable ring of fire' in Eastern Europe, North Africa, and the Middle East.[9]

EU enlargement policy may have had some flaws, but at least it was tangible and not merely declaratory; it was in line with Europe's proclaimed values, and it proved to have a pacifying effect on neighbours. It is not clear whether abandonment of this policy has saved some money and made politicians more popular with voters. However, it is fairly clear that a decade of the new Neighbourhood Policy has confronted Europe with flows of refugees, outbursts of terrorism, and a plethora of potentially explosive problems just across the porous borders. No wonder Europe's citizens feel insecure at present.

Dominant Germany and Obstinate Russia

You, Ralf, used to be more critical about your native Germany than I, a native Pole. This can partly be explained by our different life trajectories. I have not experienced Nazi rule; in Silesia, where I grew up well after the war, Germany was a symbol of efficiency and generosity despite the official Polish propaganda. In the 1970s Helmut Schmidt offered Poland generous credits for allowing native Germans from my region to rejoin their families in West Germany. Several of my German schoolmates benefited from this policy, together with numerous ordinary Poles, albeit in a different manner. I am not sure Poland's government would have been able to offer poor students like me a stipend to complete a university education without the German injection of cash at the time. After the fall of the Berlin Wall Helmut Kohl was greeted in Silesia by a huge crowd cheering under telling banners: 'Helmut, you are our chancellor!' However, Kohl resisted the temptation to redraw the post-Second World-War border with Poland. Today in Silesia Germans and Poles coexist with no major problems.

Germany has been at centre stage in the 1989 revolution. Poles are a bit envious that the beginning of the new order is identified with champagne on the Berlin Wall rather than strikes in Poland's shipyards a decade earlier. Germany has also been the greatest beneficiary of the 1989 revolution, at least in geopolitical terms. The German reunification involved a lot of money and work, but it made Germany the largest, if not the greatest, power on the continent. Even the Euro crisis has benefited Germany in some perverse ways.

With power comes responsibility, however, and this is where the critical discussion starts. Germany utilized its ever greater power for the benefit of its own citizens chiefly rather than other Europeans. It also consulted little with other Europeans over some of the fundamental decisions affecting not just Germans. This was most vivid in the summer of 2015 when Angela Merkel defied the 1990 Dublin Convention and announced that any Syrian who reaches Germany can claim asylum there. The 2012 Fiscal Compact Treaty is also seen as being imposed on other Europeans by Mrs Merkel acting in tandem with the French President Sarkozy. True, satisfying numerous European partners with their conflicting agendas was anything but easy. It is also true that playing to the domestic audience arrested the counter-revolutionary surge in Germany itself. The establishment is well in charge in the largest European country, with the Alternative for Germany party (AfD) being less popular and more moderate than the French Front National, for instance. Supporters of Mrs Merkel would add that the Fiscal Compact Treaty was an act of fiscal responsibility, while the decision regarding Syrian refugees offered Europe much-needed moral leadership.[10]

However, Merkel's critics, including those in Germany, accused her of constructing another German empire.[11] As Simon Heffer put it forcefully: 'Every spending department in every government in the Eurozone would have its policy made in the old capital of Prussia... Where Hitler failed by military means to conquer Europe, modern Germans are succeeding through trade and financial discipline. Welcome to the Fourth Reich.'[12]

Comparing Merkel to Hitler is like comparing oranges to rats. Yet, Merkel can neither ignore Germany's historical legacy nor its current might. In a 2013 Harris poll, 88 per cent of respondents in Spain, 82 per cent in Italy, and 56 per cent in France said Germany's influence in Europe is too strong. Germany's use of its power has also been questioned. Throughout the Euro crisis German policies were aimed more at punishing than assisting debtor countries. Dissenters such as the Greek (left-wing) Prime Minister Papandreou or the Italian (right-wing) Prime Minister Berlusconi were ousted on Germany's insistence. Germany has done enough to prevent the collapse of the common currency, but little to alleviate structural differences between stronger and weaker economies. Economic and fiscal policies pushed forward by Germany are producing disastrous economic, social, and political implications for debtor countries at present. Germany's desire to impose mandatory refugee quotas on the rest of the EU is also stirring up resistance. European newspapers continue to feature Angela Merkel in Nazi clothes suggesting that Germany's power represents a threat rather than a solution to Europe's current predicament.

Germany is also being blamed for the EU failures. European integration was supposed to get rid of power politics, but today new rules are being dictated by Germany and they are aimed at monitoring, policing, and punishing weaker actors. Those weaker actors include not only Cyprus, Hungary, Portugal, and Greece, but also Italy, Poland, and even France. This critical story may represent only a half-truth, but counter-revolutionary politicians point out that the deficiencies of the post-1989 system came about under German leadership, however accidentally and reluctantly.

In 1990 you, Ralf, wrote that 'Germany remains mysterious,' and I can still agree with that now. Russia is now much less mysterious than in 1990, but this does not offer any comfort, unfortunately. For the first several years after the fall of the Berlin Wall Russia was pulling back its military units from neighbouring countries. For the past several years it has been doing the opposite. The annexation of Crimea and the military support for the separatists in Donbas have made Europeans particularly concerned, but manifestations of Russia's military posturing are abundant in many other forms and places, most notably in Syria.[13]

Fear of Russia is uneven in Europe. Most concerned are the Baltic states, Romania, and Poland. They managed to convince the Americans and other NATO allies to move some of their soldiers onto their terrain. Critics argue that this move will not deter Russia, but make it more obstinate. Critics do not want to risk a confrontation with a nuclear power and undo all the work invested in overcoming the cold war legacy. Diplomacy and trade is for them the best way to handle Vladimir Putin. This may well be wishful thinking, as Putin's aggressive moves seem more driven by his domestic than international agenda. Each time Putin defies the West his popularity rises among the average Russians who otherwise have reasons to worry about the deteriorating economic condition of their country.

Russia is likely to be a major source of insecurity for some years to come with serious implications for politics in Europe. Some of Europe's citizens may care little about Crimea or Donbas, but when a civilian plane is shot down by a Russian missile used by the Donbas separatists, then the threat of Russia becomes tangible for the ordinary Dutch at least. When Russian secret services try to assassinate their defector, Alexander Litvinenko, using polonium, then Russia comes close to home for ordinary Londoners who may have been accidentally exposed to the lethal radiation. When Russian hackers, probably state sponsored, steal usernames and passwords belonging to 500 million private email addresses a cyber-war with Russia becomes a concern of not just secret services, but ordinary computer users in Europe.

Allegations that Russia finances some of Europe's counter-revolutionary parties and tries to influence electoral outcomes in Europe add to the already huge uncertainty and confusion.

In the coming years insecurity is also likely to be fuelled by Turkey. Unlike Russia, Turkey is a NATO member and a candidate for EU membership. Millions of Turks live and work in Europe. For many years, Turkey was seen as a stabilizing bridge between Europe and the Middle East. Turkey was even viewed as a model of Muslim democracy during the first years of Recep Tayyip Erdoğan's presidency. A failed military coup in 2016 and the subsequent iron fist response of Erdoğan has transformed Turkey into a major security flashpoint. The 2017 referendum gave President Erdoğan sweeping new powers, but the two main opposition parties have challenged the results. A possible civil war in Turkey is likely to spill over into countries with sizeable Turkish populations, such as Germany or Holland. A dispute between the EU and Turkey is likely to bury Europe's blueprint for containing migration. President Erdoğan's rapprochement with President Putin will cast doubts on Turkey's NATO credentials.

The list of potentially destabilizing actors should also include the United States of America, Europe's long-standing principal ally. Donald Trump in his electoral campaign questioned some basic liberal pillars of the Trans-Atlantic alliance: free trade, open borders, multilateral diplomacy, human rights, and even European integration. It is unclear whether he will change his views while in office, but it is clear that collective defence and deterrence can only work if they are not subject to speculation. Trump wants to keep his options open when it comes to the defence of Europe. Such an everything-goes policy is a recipe for anarchy, not security. I am not even talking about Trump's alleged links with Vladimir Putin.

For many European liberals the reaction to the election of Donald Trump in America was one of shock bordering on disbelief. A poll published in February 2017 by the German newspaper *Die Welt* found that only 22 per cent of Germans believe that the United States is a trustworthy ally, down from 59 per cent just three months earlier, prior to Trump's victory.[14] Yet European liberals have been left in the cold by American presidents many times before. Only a few years ago President George W. Bush drew Europeans into wars which were conducted by utterly illiberal means and with profound destabilizing implications. And we should not forget that these atrocious wars were launched under the banner of freedom.

No Order, but Confusion

Security is always a matter of degree. There is nothing like absolute security. Security is a function of many different factors. Foreign and local predators are obviously the usual suspects, but insecurity is also fuelled by ineffective government, strategic confusion, moral ambivalence, and media-generated hype. Security is also a matter of perceptions. Not all cases of violence make people feel equally insecure. Many more Europeans died in road accidents in recent years than in military combats or terrorist attacks. Yet, in an atmosphere of collective nervous breakdown such as in France after a series of terrorist attacks, it is hard for ordinary citizens to feel secure.

The main security problem of today is that we do not know who is an enemy and who is a friend. We do not know what kind of violence can soon occur and where. We do not really know which factors generate different types of insecurity. Globalization seems to threaten our jobs, identity, democracy, and even personal security, as exemplified by the fear of migrants. But do we really know what globalization means, where it leads to, and who is at its helm? No wonder weird speculations abound. As Beppe Grillo from the Five Stars Movement put it: 'The Third World War is already on its way...It is not being fought on any battle-ground with bombs, but in editorial boards of newspapers, in television stations, in top floor bank offices, in rating agencies, in multinational firms.'[15]

We are being told that the major threat is now a hybrid warfare, but do we really know what this mysterious blend of conventional and unconventional warfare signifies? The distinction between domestic and international security is blurred and so is the distinction between organized and spontaneous violence, with or without a clear political cause. States or recognized terrorist cells are not the only predators to be feared. Desperate individuals with no military training or institutional network can kill many people too, as manifested by Anders Breivik's massacre in Norway. In short, Europe's security is in a state of confusion with no credible solutions to make Europeans feel safe. This is a perfect ground for stirring up public hysteria, for searching for convenient scapegoats, and for questioning the ruling elite's capacity to govern. The more threats are hybrid, if not mysterious, the more we fear them. As Zygmunt Bauman observed: 'Fear is at its most fearsome when it is diffuse, scattered, unclear, unattached, unanchored, free floating, with no clear address or cause; when it haunts us with no visible rhyme or reason, when the menace we should be afraid of can be glimpsed everywhere but is nowhere to be seen.'[16]

Of course, the post-1989 elite cannot be blamed for everything that went wrong. Some of the security problems relate to technological change; cyber attacks were unknown in the pre-1989 era, for instance. Other problems result from long-term socio-cultural processes beyond Europe's influence; Muslim fundamentalism in North Africa and the Middle East has chiefly local roots, for instance. However, the post-1989 security regime has been designed and implemented in a manner subject to criticism. No wonder the counter-revolutionary politicians are able to exploit the growing feeling of insecurity.

The pre-1989 security system in Europe was unjust, but it was fairly stable. The Soviet threat was imminent, but it was neutralized by a sound nuclear deterrence posture and the unambiguous 'first strike' doctrine. Military budgets were high, but generals knew what was needed for a clearly defined scenario of a possible conflict. The collapse of the Soviet empire produced what liberals had always wanted: a Europe 'whole and free'. The side effects of this noble achievement were fuzzy borders, interconnection, and interdependence. Destabilization and misinformation have become more potent in this interconnected environment. They can be practised not just by states such as Russia, but also by terrorist groups such as so-called ISIS. It is now fairly easy to stir up public unrest across borders by fabricating stories of injustice.[17] Disrupting trade and investments becomes a common international practice. As Mark Leonard put it eloquently: 'Mutually Assured Disruption is the new MAD.'[18]

With the collapse of the Berlin Wall and the old security order there was an obvious need for self-reflection and self-constraint. The opposite has happened. Proposals to create a new pan-European security architecture were never taken on board by defence and foreign ministers; instead, NATO and EU enlargements progressed making the Russian elite increasingly uneasy. Freed from Cold War constraints Europeans began to use their military forces with relative ease, first in the Balkans and then in the Middle East. The moral arguments used for these military actions were dubious at best. Is killing the best way to prevent killing? Can moral aims be achieved by using 'immoral' violent means? There was much talk about multilateralism, but some British and French military adventures could not even gather the support of fellow Europeans. Above all, most of these military interventions have failed to achieve their proclaimed aims. Some even made the security situation worse, not just for the states being shelled, but also for Europeans themselves. There are solid grounds to believe that these military interventions generated migratory waves and made Europe a target of Islamic terrorists. What have the governments in question done to prepare for these side effects of military adventures? They can hardly claim to be surprised by them.

The legacy of the 1989 revolution is thus a sweeping disorder generating insecurity. 'At the very moment when world order is more liberal than it ever was,' reflected Georg Sørensen, 'both the economic and the political dimension of liberal order are in crisis.'[19] This has partly been caused by a strategic confusion and intellectual impotence. European liberals prided themselves on promoting emancipation, justice, democracy, and development, but they never abandoned the politics of power and profit. They tried to pursue incompatible policy aims such as humanitarian aid, peacekeeping, and peace enforcement, usually with little enthusiasm, or money. They relied on international institutions which have been detached from ordinary citizens geographically and culturally, rewarded financial firms and corporate lawyers at the expense of consumers, and grabbed ever more powers without being subject to any meaningful public scrutiny. As Jeff D. Colgan and Robert O. Keohane rightly argued, liberals have constructed international institutions 'in a biased way' and 'underestimated the risk that [they] posed'. This is why 'some portion of the blame for the liberal order's woes lies with its advocates'.[20]

The liberal vision of the world order was noble, but vague. Trade and multilateral diplomacy may well have a pacifying effect in the long term, but they are not a panacea for all kinds of immediate security threats and risks. Yet, liberals never properly explained to the public what their key security objectives are and how they are going to implement them. If the main threat comes from terrorism, why should a state invest in super-expensive nuclear submarines?[21] If Russia represents an imminent threat will a thousand American soldiers in Poland represent a deterrent?[22] And will banning burkinis on Europe's beaches prevent terrorist attacks?[23] Officials argue that all of these measures are making us safer to some degree. The problem is that they do not form a coherent, let alone plausible, strategy. Post-1989 governments have usually responded to violent incidents or threats in an ad hoc, chaotic manner.

An 'anything goes' policy that shifts from one position to another is hardly efficient and reassuring. Counter-revolutionary politicians may well offer simplistic solutions to complex security problems, but the post-1989 elite lacks a plausible paradigm helping people to get out of the security maze. Europe's security policy resembles a famous passage from T. S. Eliot: 'Time yet for a hundred indecisions | And for a hundred visions and revisions, | Before taking a toast and tea.'[24] This is what the counter-revolutionary politicians expose and criticize. They do not need to do much more to succeed.

6

BARBARIANS AT THE GATE

Ralf, you and I have been migrants for most of our lives. This made us think about migration in biased, personal terms. White international academics like us were seldom harassed by immigration or police officers but all migrants have experienced some form of discrimination, real or imagined. All migrants have struggled with their foreign accents and manners. All migrants have encountered the suspicion and prejudices of some local colleagues and neighbours. All migrants have worried about their complicated legal status. You do not need to resemble the archetype of a Muslim terrorist to feel uneasy in a European tube, school, or sports club.

Migrants' experiences are not all negative. Despite possible frustrations with the host country, migrants tend to develop an affectionate relationship with their new place. You once told me about your love affair with Great Britain, which started in 1948 at Wilton Park near Shoreham-by-Sea. Since at the time you were undergoing a 're-education' with German PoWs, the circumstances of your love affair were quite peculiar. Later you even became a supporter of Arsenal football club, the same way I became a passionate supporter of Ajax Amsterdam during my Dutch spell, and even more so of Fiorentina after moving to Italy.

Migrants know the meaning of borders and the difference between open and closed ones. I will never forget my first trip through a divided Berlin. Ruthless East German border guards were pointing their machine guns at everyone in the train compartment and their dogs were barking obsessively at those searched. For me the greatest gain after 1989 was the ability to visit my native country free from fear and restrictions. Having a Schengen (Dutch) passport facilitated travel all over the world, not only within the EU.

Not all migrants ended up with a Schengen passport, however. Many of them have been deported back to their countries, sometimes after many years of legal struggle or living underground in an adopted country. The motives for migration vary and so do the circumstances of individual migrants. Some migrants flee wars while others flee unemployment. Some of Europe's most successful artists, academics, and entrepreneurs are migrants, but poverty and even slavery is a more common fate of migrants. The current political discourse tends to paint all migrants with one broad brush, ignoring personal histories and dreams. Yet, migration is always about personal, emotional stories, which defy simple narratives or statistics.

The attitude of local people towards migrants is also more about emotions and symbols than about interests and facts. It has always been like that. Migration is part of human history and politics towards migrants was hardly ever realpolitik. It was about addressing prejudices and fears. It was about handling the strange other; barbarians, as they used to be called. Before the first Opium War, a member of the Grand Secretariat of the Imperial Manchu Court in China, Wei Yuan, was asked to prepare a document on how to handle European migrants. His advice was simple: 'In order to handle barbarian affairs, you have to know barbarian sentiments; in order to know barbarian sentiments, you have to know barbarian conditions.'[1] I wish this logic would prevail in contemporary Europe when handling migrants, though without the barbarian label.

Refugee Crisis

It would be wrong to assume that anti-migrant sentiments are all about xenophobia and racism. They are in part, if not chiefly, evoked by the dysfunctional system of handling migration. They are rooted in hostility to the ideal of open borders endorsed by the liberal establishment. This vision of Europe without fences and walls has in any event been applied unevenly by liberal governments. Wealthy entrepreneurs could cross borders much more easily than poor jobseekers and political refugees. This kept anti-migration sentiments under control. However, when more than one million refugees crossed Europe's borders in 2015–16 the counter-revolutionary politicians seized their chance. Their long-standing critique of the liberal vision of open borders and of the poor management of these borders started to gain wider public support. The Muslim origin of many refugees has made them easy targets of cultural and religious prejudices. A series of terrorist attacks across Europe committed by Islamic extremists have naturally contributed to the public anxiety. Bashing migration became the most potent weapon of the anti-liberal uprising.

The refugee crisis has also undermined another long-standing pillar of liberalism: respect for human rights and citizenship. As Hannah Arendt and Giorgio Agamben argued, these two values are not about the same things, and liberals were happier to grant refugees human rights than political rights in the form of citizenship. This obviously helped the counter-revolutionaries treat a refugee as the other, inferior entity. Moreover, with any huge exodus of desperate people fleeing war and misery, liberals struggled to treat single refugees as genuine humans. Refugees became a mass phenomenon to be dealt with in an institutional manner, and there was little willingness and ability to consider each single refugee as an individual with a particular history and rights. In fact, policies to prevent people from fleeing their countries openly denied refugees their human rights. The most striking example of this was the EU decision to abandon the operation Mare Nostrum, which aimed to prevent refugees from drowning in the Mediterranean Sea. The official argument was that helping desperate refugees to survive encouraged others to head towards Europe. According to the International Organization for Migration, more than 3,770 migrants were reported to have died trying to cross the Mediterranean in 2015, and over 5,000 in 2016, but this has not deterred desperate people fleeing their countries.

Liberals have claimed that their betrayal of liberal values is justified by an unprecedented situation. Yet, none of this was unprecedented. The First and Second World Wars caused much greater migrations and there was hardly any effective governance then. Displacements and resettlements due to the Indian partition, the Indochina wars, the war in Yugoslavia, or ethnic migration of Germans from the Soviet Union have also been greater in scale than the recent refugee wave in Europe.[2] This most recent refugee influx represented just a small proportion of the much larger processes of forced displacement of over 20 million people in the vicinity of the EU and 60 million worldwide. The EU's population increased 0.2 per cent as a result of the recent refugee influx. In comparison, Turkey's population increased by 4 per cent, and Lebanon's by 25 per cent, both countries less affluent than the average member of the EU.[3]

Horrific scenes at the Keleti rail station in Budapest were not unprecedented either, even by modern European standards. They resembled scenes from Brindisi port in 1991 after the arrival of a ship with 20,000 Albanians. The Italian filmmaker, Daniele Vicari, has documented the latter events in his acclaimed film *La Nave Dolce* (*The Human Cargo*).[4] Policy-makers should start their training on migration by watching Vicari's documentary.

The majority of recent refugees, in absolute terms, ended up in Germany and, in relative terms, in Sweden, yet these were not the countries with the greatest anti-refugee sentiments. In Poland manifestations of anti-Islamic and anti-refugee phobias have been particularly vicious even though the country hosts only a handful of Islamic asylum seekers from Chechnya and practically no Afghans or Syrians. Poland hosts one million Ukrainian migrants, many of them fleeing violence in its eastern part, and yet anti-Ukrainian sentiments have not been pronounced in Poland. Clearly the fear of barbarians is not necessarily the result of any direct encounters.

Counter-revolutionary rhetoric has often stirred up public hysteria, manifested most clearly when refugees are portrayed as terrorists. As Viktor Orbán put it succinctly: 'all the terrorists are basically migrants.'[5] In fact, most of the terrorist acts recently committed on European soil were by people born in Europe. It is also true that some of them could exploit the chaos on Europe's borders to move back and forth between continents by posing as refugees. For instance, it was confirmed that the Belgian national of Moroccan origin, Abdelhamid Abaaoud, who organized the Paris attacks that killed 129 people in November 2015, had travelled through Greece with a large group of refugees and migrants from North Africa and the Middle East.

This leads us to the border-management question. Europe's liberal leaders promised a comprehensive, coherent, humane, and effective management of refugees that addressed the root causes and not only symptoms of the problem. In reality their policies did the opposite, making things worse rather than better. Military interventions conducted by Europeans and Americans in Afghanistan and the Middle East killed thousands of innocent civilians and contributed to the instability that generated migration. Most of Europe's countries failed to live up to their development aid pledges and their post-conflict state-building efforts were either limited or absent altogether. During the Arab Spring Europe did not rush to help democratic campaigners even in such relatively successful cases as Tunisia. Most of Europe's money went to autocrats promising to control their outward migration, with limited tangible results, however. Patrolling maritime space between Europe and North Africa has also failed to bring about promised results. Closing one route of migration simply opened another one. When a greater than usual number of desperate people decided to head northwards, Europe's officials looked totally surprised, itself surprising given the gap between their rhetoric and behaviour.

Under the so-called Dublin Regulation, refugees had to apply for asylum in the first EU country they entered, and if they crossed borders to another country after being fingerprinted they could be returned to the former. This put disproportionate burdens on countries such as Greece or Italy; they were neither able nor willing to enforce this regulation when faced with larger refugee waves. And since people could move freely within the Schengen zone, the Dublin Regulation remained a piece of paper. When Hungary decided to enforce this regulation in 2015 it led to the horrifying scenes witnessed on TV screens and mobile phones all over the world.

Germany has subsequently decided to suspend compliance with the Dublin Regulation and voluntarily assumed responsibility for processing all Syrian asylum applications within its borders. Angela Merkel probably realized that Germany cannot treat refugees in an inhumane manner as Hungary did, if only because of the parallels to the East German and Nazi practices. The German decision has been criticized for being taken with little or no consultation with the governments of Hungary, Slovakia, and Poland, in particular. Governments of these countries also refused to endorse mandatory quotas for distributing refugees among EU member states. A desperate Merkel has subsequently negotiated a deal with Turkey: in return for taking back migrants that have 'illegally' reached Greece from Turkey, the EU has promised to pay Turkey to support refugee camps; open a new chapter in the EU accession talks; and offer Turkish citizens visa-free travel into the European Union. In the first several months following the agreement the number of refugees reaching Greece via Turkey has indeed reduced, but the number of refugees reaching Italy via the Mediterranean Sea has increased. So, in the summer of 2017 we have witnessed another flurry of EU meetings trying to cope with refugees, with no tangible results. Italy was left alone to cope with refugees heading for its shores, and refugees were left to the mercy of weather, traffickers, and humanitarian NGOs. When the Mediterranean floating 'cemetery' began to break the record of new 'arrivals,' Europe's leaders rushed to Libya with bribes for local warlords in exchange of sealing off the coastal border. Such deals proved ineffective in the past and they profoundly tainted Europe's liberal image.

The chances of Turkey joining the EU are slim if only because the government in Ankara openly defies some basic European standards, especially after the 2016 failed military coup trying to oust President Erdoğan. Even visa-free travel between the EU and Turkey is in doubt. In this situation one wonders whether the EU–Turkey deal will last. Nor is it certain that Turkey would be able to halt the refugee tide even if it wanted to. There are multiple violent conflicts just beyond Turkish borders and refugee camps in Turkey are already in a dire condition.

It looks as though Europe will face refugee flows for many years to come. The prospect that wars and misery in North Africa and the Middle East will end soon are nil. Even the enormous death toll in the Mediterranean Sea failed to deter people fleeing their troubled countries. The deal with Turkey is fragile, and so is the one with Libyan leaders. Hastily erected walls and wire fences at different locations in Europe have few practical consequences. European governments are in vain trying to find some common ground to cope with refugees. Their policies are progressively illiberal and they are not effective. In some countries xenophobic mobs have attacked refugees and burned down the facilities of humanitarian NGOs helping refugees. In most countries electorates have begun to endorse counter-revolutionary parties campaigning with anti-refugee slogans. Not only migrants from Muslim countries are under fire; migration from other European countries is also being questioned.

Facts and Fiction

Disturbing images of refugees from Kos island in Greece or the Hungarian-Serbian border made many think that migration is chiefly caused by wars in Europe's troubled neighbourhoods. This is not always the case, however. In Ireland the largest group of migrants are British, in Spain and Italy Romanians, in Austria Germans. In other countries non-EU migrants represent the largest group; in France Algerians, in Britain Indians, in Germany Turks, and in Poland Ukrainians. The picture is very mixed indeed.

France and Great Britain, in contrast to Germany and Sweden, have been only marginally affected by the recent refugee flow. Britain had the most immigrants for the purpose of work and study; less than 5 per cent of migrants ask for asylum in Great Britain. In France the largest group of those immigrating is the group joining family or entering schools. France is also one of those few European countries where migration has decreased in recent years.

Law makes a distinction between migrants seeking political asylum and those coming for other purposes. The public discourse simplifies this dichotomy a bit and talks about political and economic migrants. Yet, the border between various groups of migrants is fuzzy in practice. The motivations and situations of individual migrants are seldom simple. Many people flee not because they are persecuted by their governments, but because their governments are unable to cope with local violence, climate change, or food shortages. They are neither typical economic nor political migrants, but form a new and ever larger group of 'survival migrants', to use Alexander Betts's words.[6]

Immigrants stay for varying lengths of time, with some becoming permanent residents, while others shuttle between their country of origin and the new country. The nationality, education, and culture of migrants determine their legal status, labour skills, and assimilation into local communities. In short, there is no simple way to classify migrants; by the same token, one-size-fits-all policies towards migration cannot apply here.

Attitudes to immigration are also complex and difficult to measure. According to Eurobarometer data, the UK records relatively high levels of concern over time and France relatively low levels. In Germany, Syrians have been welcomed by ordinary citizens with flowers, but the statistical data for the last two years show a huge increase in the percentage of Germans who see migration as a top issue facing their country.

Data show that anxiety about migration stems from numerous sources, but security, economic, and cultural concerns seem most pronounced.[7] PEW Research Global Attitudes Survey of 2016 found that the biggest fear associated with refugees is the fear of terrorism. Interestingly, economic fears have been more pronounced in France where the deadliest terrorist acts have been committed lately.

Cultural fears are difficult to quantify. The IPSOS Mori Global Advisor poll of 2016 asked people whether immigration is causing their country to change in ways they don't like and many of them answered in the affirmative, especially in France (more than 50 per cent). An unfavourable view of Muslim immigrants has been particularly pronounced in several polls, although it has decreased in recent years in countries such as Germany and Sweden.

Cultural fears may well be difficult to quantify, but they are being exploited quite skilfully by counter-revolutionary politicians. As Marine Le Pen put it: 'Immigration is an organized replacement of our population. This threatens our very survival. We don't have the means to integrate those who are already here. The result is endless cultural conflict.'[8] Economic fears related to migration are easier to measure, but they are confusing nevertheless. Statistics usually point to pressure placed by migrants on jobs and social benefits of the hosting countries. This notwithstanding, other data point to gaps in the labour market being filled by migrants and the overall financial benefits stemming from migration. Low or even negative demographic growth in most European countries may require migrants from outside Europe to keep the welfare system sustainable in the long term. Of course, long-term calculations may not influence citizens' perceptions of migration, and financial benefits do not necessarily reward those living in areas affected by migration. The data also show that people who are most concerned about immigration are often the people living in areas least affected by it.

All the confusing statistics aside, one thing is fairly clear: across Europe people are dissatisfied with the way governments manage immigration of various kinds. The number of migrants has steadily gone up in Europe despite governmental assurances to reverse or arrest this trend. This is partly because migration is not easy to control, let alone to halt. States continue to pursue the politically expedient fiction that they can unilaterally assert sovereign control over immigration but the reality is more complex. For instance, the majority of immigrants cross borders legally and stay on after their visas expire. Curbing that sort of migration would require major restrictions of international travel and the introduction of mass police surveillance on all residents.

Moreover, governments who talk tough about migration for political reasons act soft on migration for economic reasons. Migrants not only perform jobs that the local population is unwilling to perform, they are also willing to work on terms that the local population is unwilling to accept (and has the legal ground to do so). Neo-liberal economics would not be able to achieve its aim of having cheaper and less protected labour without migrants. In this sense the migration policy of numerous European states can be called a systemic pretence.

Hypocrisy and pretence have their price, and Great Britain is a very good example. After the 2004 EU enlargement most Western European governments utilized a seven-year transition period in order to prepare for an inflow of new migrants from Eastern Europe. Great Britain decided to welcome Eastern Europeans instantly to fill the gaps in the labour market and stimulate economic growth. The number of EU workers subsequently increased from 2.6 per cent to 6.8 per cent over a decade, most of them coming from Poland and other new EU member states. This influx of labour has clearly helped Britain to get out of the recession and to create extra jobs for Brits too.[9]

Yet, those places with the highest concentration of new foreign labour have experienced a 'cultural shock' and seen overcrowded hospitals and schools. According to experts, the government was more skilful in collecting taxes from new migrants than in investing in local infrastructure aimed at easing pressures on social services. Instead of admitting its mistakes, the government began to blame the EU for the influx of foreign labour and the immigrant labour for exploiting the British social welfare system. The latter claim was never backed by any evidence.[10] The HMRC figures show that migrants who arrived in Britain since 2011 from the EU paid £2.5 billion more in tax and national insurance than they took in tax credits and child benefits. The Pandora's box was opened, however. Anti-immigration feelings have become widespread leading to the surge in support for UKIP and the 'yes' vote in the Brexit referendum. The latter has generated a political earthquake in Britain with unknown implications. The economic costs of Brexit are also unknown, but they clearly exceed the costs of addressing local social problems created by the influx of Polish or Lithuanian labour.

The UK's model of growth is heavily dependent not just on trade, but also on the open labour market. Economists from Kings College London, Jonathan Portes and Giuseppe Forte, found that 'the potential negative impact of Brexit-induced reductions in openness to migration on the UK economy could well equal that resulting from Brexit-induced reductions in trade'.[11]

Public anxiety evoked by the continuous influx of new migrants is understandable. Migration is on the rise for various reasons and its benefits are not obvious for large parts of the population. It is also true that politicians have tried to exploit the migration issue for their partisan political aims. Misinformation, manipulation, and the blame game became the order of the day in public discourse, fuelling extreme views and political passions.

Counter-revolutionary politicians proved more skilful in this chaotic environment. The establishment was forced onto the defensive and began introducing policies that contradicted its proclaimed liberal principles. With time liberals began to look like a softer version of their anti-liberal opponents; the difference between them was rhetoric and style, but not the substance of anti-migrant policies. As always the picture differed depending on local circumstances and the actors involved. Some politicians who see themselves as liberal, such as Nicholas Sarkozy, adopted an anti-immigrant stance similar to their counter-revolutionary opponents, while politicians seen as illiberal, such as Alexis Tsipras, tried to treat migrants in a humane way. Angela Merkel was praised by human rights campaigners for welcoming Syrian refugees, but criticized for her deal with Turkey which set aside human rights concerns.

Given the complexity of the matter, the divergence of views surrounding it, and the scale of emotions involved, migration is likely to remain a hot political battleground in Europe. As Simon Jenkins rightly observed: 'Migration is a fact of life—yet our deluded leaders try to turn back the tide . . . We should learn to handle it, not pretend to stop it.'[11]

However, there is not one solution, let alone a simple one, for handling migration in an effective and humane manner. Politicians should therefore present different options to their voters and try to gain their support. The assumption that the public will always support xenophobes is in my view unfounded. Yet, the public is likely to punish politicians who promise to stop migration but promote a type of economics that cannot do without a continuous influx of cheap migrant labour. It would be naive to assume that the majority of Europeans are ready to welcome refugees into their homes, but this does not mean that they expect the government to shoot all those attempting to cross borders illegally. It is one thing to allow Eastern Europeans to work legally in Northern England, quite another to tolerate slave labour in the plantation fields of Calabria. Some voters may prefer machines rather than migrants nursing patients in Europe's hospitals. (Japan has already embarked on this course.) Yet, politicians cannot treat citizens as passive consumers of their propaganda. Politicians should have the expertise and courage to present their own remedies for a different kind of migration. We are not talking here about a better narrative on migration; we are talking about a genuine dialogue with the public on this sensitive subject. Liberal politicians must and can demonstrate that their solutions are more effective than those supported by the counter-revolutionary insurgents. Bashing all Islamists indiscriminately implies that extremists are given shelter among ordinary Muslim citizens of Holland, Belgium, France, or Germany. Bashing Polish migrants will cost the United Kingdom access to the single market. What kind of practical deal is it?

Embracing soft populism does not make liberals look credible in the eyes of the public. Proposing simple solutions to complex migratory problems is not likely to convince anyone, especially in the long term. Yet, liberals have done this time and again. They tried to make people believe that naval ships can stop migration, that bribing dictators will seal North African coasts, that sending food and tents to refugees' camps in the Middle East and Africa will make refugees stay there forever, that migration in such different countries as Sweden, France, Hungary, and Greece requires one single European remedy. As home secretary, Theresa May sent vans bearing the slogan 'Go home' into areas of high immigration. What did she want to achieve by that?

We can discuss whether the aforementioned 'practical' policies were liberal, but it is obvious that they were not very effective, and at times they were also counterproductive. They made liberals appear to be not merely feeble populists, but incompetent chumps. When faced with criticism, liberals immediately cried foul. Anyone who disagreed with them was denounced as intolerant and bigoted. This has made the work of counter-revolutionary politicians that much easier. Nigel Farage has described the 'go home' campaign on vans as 'nasty' which tells us something about the muddle liberals found themselves in.[12]

Pragmatic versus Moral Positions

Like you, Ralf, I prefer a discussion about practical solutions to real problems without engaging in moralism. If a certain type of migration is considered a threat, let's consider the nature and scale of this threat. Let's talk about all possible measures to mitigate or even end the unwanted type of migration. Threats are always a matter of degree. We cannot spend our lives in bunkers only because our streets are not perfectly safe. There are a variety of pragmatic measures to deal with refugees and migrants: those which are peaceful and those which are violent. Given that the current migration discourse is dominated by emotions, myths, and lies, a certain dose of pragmatism would already represent some progress. I fear, however, that we cannot escape from moral stances when dealing with migrants. The point is not only to refrain from inhumane treatment of migrants, but to enforce our standards of humanity in practice. Benign neglect will not do. This is a lesson from history. In 1934 at the Evian refugee conference and again in 1944 at the Bermuda conference the international community failed to rescue the German and later Balkan Jews from Nazi persecution. We know the implications of this benign neglect.

Benign neglect does not only concern politicians, but also ordinary people. In his 2015 diary reporting visits to Keleti train station in Budapest, Béla Greskovits, described the horrific conditions of refugees waiting there; a 'labyrinth of hell,' as he put it: a single open water pipe with six taps and seven toilets for thousands of refugees, for instance. Greskovits compared this devastating experience with the situation just two metro stations away where locals and tourists gathered in open-air restaurants and pubs with music. '"Normal" life is going on—next to the seas of suffering,' reflected Greskovits.

> This is perhaps the same as it ever was. In the Spring and Summer of 1944, when Hungarian Jews were forced into ghettos to wait there for the trains taking them to the gas chambers of Auschwitz, Hungarian theatres played Lehár's or Kálmán's operettas, Verdi's operas, jazz arrived to in Budapest, people went to cinemas, kids to schools, workers to the factories, and Christians to service. Some people with good hearts visited the ghetto and brought food, drinks, and other much-needed items. For a while everything seemed 'normal'—while in the final account everything had been profoundly abnormal.[13]

The current abnormal situation is caused by politicians coming from many different parties, not just those labelled populist. Voters supporting these politicians and parties are also implicated. The distinction between liberal and illiberal politics is of little meaning here. The crucial distinction is between humanity and barbarity. You can guess, Ralf, who are barbarians in Greskovits' sad story. We do not want to see our countries being run by barbarians with no human compass whatsoever. We do not want our citizens to lose basic human instincts either.

7

THE RISE AND FALL
OF THE EU

European integration used to be a jewel in the liberal crown.
Integration was not only seen as a quintessential liberal project,
but also as a tool for spreading liberal values in Europe and beyond.
The embodiment of integration—the European Union—was declared
a symbol of peace, prosperity, and opportunity on the Continent. The
EU was seen as an effective instrument for handling globalization,
a courageous experiment in transnational democracy, a clever way of
stabilizing neighbours, and a vehicle for strengthening Europe's global
position. In 2005 Mark Leonard eloquently explained 'why Europe
will run the 21st century' and he was praised by a chorus of liberal
commentators.[1]

Less than a decade later bashing the EU and the integration project
has proved to be the surest way of gaining votes for the counter-
revolutionaries. Local counter-revolutionary groupings are divided on
many policy issues, but they are remarkably united in their opposition
to the EU, its leaders, laws, and policies. They see the EU as bureau-
cratic, undemocratic, and detached from the concerns of ordinary
citizens. They accuse the EU of being an agent of globalization, shed-
ding jobs, and curbing social benefits. They interpret the EU cosmopolitan culture as offensive towards national and religious feelings.
They blame the EU for generating and tolerating unsustainable waves
of migration. The EU's 'porous' borders are seen by the counter-
revolutionaries as benefiting terrorists and ordinary criminals. The
EU is even held responsible for the war in Ukraine and instability in

the Middle East and North Africa. In short, curbing the powers of the EU or leaving the EU or the Eurozone altogether is recommended as the best way to regain prosperity and security for individual European states. The counter-revolutionaries assume or hope that the end of the EU will imply the end of the liberal era. They promise a new glorious history built on the ashes of the integration project. More and more people are tempted to believe this anti-European narrative, and not just in the United Kingdom. In fact, the greatest drop in support for the EU can be observed in countries traditionally pro-European such as Greece, Italy, and Spain.

How can we explain this dramatic shift in the public opinion? Why is the EU no longer so popular even among experts? As Andrew Moravcsik pointed out in 2017, numerous statistical data still suggest that the EU either rivals or surpasses the United States and China in its economic, diplomatic, and even military capacity.[2] Why is this not appreciated by so many Europeans? Why can't Europe's aggregate potential be transformed into a common purposeful project shared by most Europeans?

The most obvious reply would point to the flaws of the liberal project described in this letter. If liberalism and European integration are intertwined, the former conditions the latter. Alternative explanations ought to be considered, however. Perhaps Europe embarked on a misguided model of integration from the get-go. Perhaps it failed to adjust to geopolitical and societal changes. Perhaps the institutions of integration have been half-built and collapsed under pressure from external shocks. Perhaps the EU has become an agent of disintegration at odds with the liberal creed. Perhaps integration was not a good idea in the first place. All of these suppositions have some merit, with the exception of the last one, I will argue.

Liberal Roots

European integration was inspired by several key liberal propositions shared not only by liberal, but also by Christian democratic and social democratic parties since 1945. Liberals always believed that open markets are the best means of generating wealth and opportunities, of challenging vested interests, and of expanding people's freedom. The most prominent liberals, such as John Stuart Mill, even held that trade generates peace because trade requires collaboration, trust, and openness.[3] Trade also generates economic interdependence or even mutual vulnerability which liberals see as positive things because they create a common destiny of states and people. Liberals thought that common laws and institutions enhance cooperation and help to settle potential conflicts. A certain kind of central authority is also required not just to arrest free riding, but also to aggregate power and steer it towards collective ends. Not all liberals were nomads (Immanuel Kant hardly ever left Königsberg), but they were internationalists fiercely combating pathologies of nationalism.

The experience of two horrible wars in the twentieth century reinforced this normative thinking. Security based on walls, deterrence, and balance of power resulted in millions of deaths and economic destruction. The absolute notion of sovereignty emphasizing national economics and jurisdiction seemed at odds with the post-war concept of modernity. Economic integration and transnational regulation was seen not just as a means for boosting growth and prosperity, but also for diffusing security concerns. The Schuman Declaration of 1950 stated that the European Coal and Steel Community, a forerunner of the EU, is to make war between historic rivals 'not merely unthinkable, but materially impossible'.[4]

There is no point in speculating what post-war Europe would have been like without the EC/EU. While it is true that many different factors have contributed to peace and prosperity, European integration was certainly one of them. This was even recognized by the Tory government in the early 1970s which saw joining the EC as a means of enhancing British well-being. The June 1970 speech of Anthony Barber, a UK government spokesman, outlining the British position towards the common market unambiguously declared: 'It is wholly unrealistic to separate the political and economic interests of Europe, because our place in the world, and our influence, will be largely determined by the growth of our resources and the pace of our technological development. Economic growth and technological development today require that we integrate our economies and our markets.'[5] Archives revealing private discussions within the British government four decades ago confirm that politicians could hardly see their country booming while remaining outside Europe's integrative scheme. This is history, however, at least as far as British Tories are concerned.

It is difficult to establish when things started to go wrong in Europe. Specialists in economics point to the collapse of the Bretton Woods system and the subsequent oil crisis that slowed down Europe's impressive economic growth. Specialists in geopolitics point to the fall of communism in Eastern Europe which put the European project under enormous stress. The EU has enlarged dramatically, Germany has become not only larger, but also more powerful, and new neighbours have generated instability and migration. Specialists in EU institutions point to the failure of the European Constitution as a result of negative referenda in the Netherlands and France. Major reforms of the EU have been difficult if not impossible since.

Whatever the reasons for Europe's worsening condition the last decade has seen the EU generating opposite effects from those originally intended. The EU's major rationale was always efficiency, not citizens' participation. Its case rested on the modernist notion of competence and progress rather than traditional notions of loyalty, trust, or affection. Nation-states, unlike the EU, had their mythical long history and democratic mechanisms connecting them with citizens. Yet, they were too small and weak to cope with global commercial, migratory, or security pressures. Because of its impressive size and scale the EU was able to accomplish things that individual states were not. Would any European state be able to impose and execute a mega fine of $1.4bn for failure to comply with anti-competitive business practices on a giant such as Microsoft? This is what the EU has actually accomplished.

True, European decision-making was always complex, slow, and hostage to the lowest common denominator, but this has not prevented the EU from flexing its muscle within and outside its borders. Consider the skilful way of stabilizing Central and Eastern Europe after the fall of the Soviet system through the policy of enlargement under strict conditions. Or think about the European Commission and the European Court of Justice's impressive capacity to enforce application of the *acquis communautaire* comprising some 20,000 European laws, decisions, and regulations. However, today the European institutions look paralysed and unable to make progress on the most pressing issues. Individual member states practice cherry-picking in complying with European norms and laws, while the EU Neighbourhood Policy amounts to empty declarations. After three successive bailouts and numerous EU summits hardly anybody believes that Greece will ever pay its debts. Nor is it credible to claim that several EU summits devoted to economic migrants and political refugees have found a durable, let alone ethical, solution for coping with them. Russia is not going to leave Crimea, despite the EU sanctions. The EU is not even able to steer global trade and environmental negotiations, something that used to be the EU's speciality.

One can go even a step further and argue that most of the problems Europe is facing at present have been generated by the EU itself. This is because the Euro was designed in a deficient way, and so was the Schengen system. I am not even talking about the European Common Foreign and Security Policy, which never had any meaningful diplomatic and military means at its disposal. In short, the EU institutions seem no longer fit for purpose, and by extension they are inefficient, undermining the basic rationale behind the EU's very existence.

European integration was also supposed to create the most competitive economy in the world. It was supposed to make the 'Stockholm consensus' prevail over the 'Washington consensus', not just in the north, but also in the east and south of Europe. The common currency and the single market were the key means for achieving these ambitious economic aims. For a long time, these objectives seemed to be fulfilled even beyond expectations. The EC/EU generated growth by enforcing rules of economic competition and by abolishing barriers to the movement of capital, goods, services, and people within its borders. It negotiated external trade agreements protecting member states from exporters using lower labour or environmental standards. It helped weaker economic actors (in the private sector such as the farmers and in the public sector such as the regions) to cope with economic pressures. It opened and transformed markets of neighbouring countries through the policy of conditional accession to the EU or through various forms of association.

Growth has been distributed more evenly in Europe than in other parts of the world, diffusing industrial conflicts and contributing to competiveness. Sweden, Finland, and Denmark with their high levels of welfare spending and environmental regulation score as well as the United States on the Global Competitiveness Index. The economies of Germany, Austria, and the Netherlands have consistently performed well despite their high taxes and social benefits. The Euro initially seemed a great success too, sheltering Europe from financial volatility and lowering costs of transactions. Today, the common currency is in trouble and it undermines the achievements of the single market. Even the strongest European economies struggle to generate growth and Europe's welfare systems are shrinking. The European Commission seems more eager to listen to 30,000 lobbyists in Brussels than to ordinary citizens across the continent. The Euro was meant to help integrate Europe, but it achieved the opposite; it exacerbated the gaps and conflicts between the surplus and deficit countries, the importers and exporters, and the north and south.

Last but not least, European integration was supposed to get rid of power politics. Large and rich states were no longer to bully small and impoverished ones. Above all, Europe was not to be ruled by Germany. Today, a few 'triple A' countries run Europe with Germany in the driving seat. Gone is equality among member states. New treaties are written with only some states in mind, external (arbitrary) interference in domestic affairs abounds, and policies are chiefly about punishment rather than assistance and incentives.

Cul-de-sac

You may argue that my description of the present-day EU is unfair, but how else one can explain the meagre public support for the EU as compared with two or three decades earlier? True, many citizens are not happy with their nation-states either, but at least they can vote their inefficient leaders out of office. This is hardly possible in the EU. In the 2014 elections to the European Parliament, parties led by Nigel Farage and Marine Le Pen came first in the United Kingdom and France respectively, beating the entire liberal establishment on the Right and Left of the political spectrum.[6] The media announced a Eurosceptic 'shock' or 'earthquake'. A triumphant Marine Le Pen told cheering supporters at Front National (FN) party headquarters in Paris, 'The people have spoken loud and clear. They no longer want to be led by those outside our borders, by EU commissioners and technocrats who are unelected.'[7]

Strikingly, Europe's liberal politicians continued with business as usual. In a moment of political delirium, they even called the selection of Jean-Claude Juncker as the European Commission President a 'triumph of democracy'. This was because Juncker was the so-called *spitzenkandidat* selected by the centre-right coalition in the European Parliament. Never mind his responsibility for such failures as the EU's heavy-handed management of the Euro crisis or the light-handed approach to tax evasion.[8] Equally puzzling was the selection of Donald Tusk as President of the European Council. Tusk prides himself on having little vision or ideology. As he put it in a 'farewell' interview for *Polityka* before leaving Warsaw for Brussels: 'I sincerely believe that common sense is always better than ideology, decency is better than vision.'[9] One cannot shed the impression that in the present-day EU, visionless technocrats dominate policy-making while visionary zealots dominate politics. This does not bode well for European integration.

I would have sounded more optimistic had the counter-revolutionary pressure led to self-reflection and self-improvement across the continent. Yet, the liberal elite is shifting between unrealistic federal plans and benign neglect. The former stipulates that the EU represents a half-built house: there are common rules, even a common currency, but without a genuine common government. The European centre is too weak to control its constitutive parts. There are good reasons why this is so, however. Putting the EU in charge of economic supervision, taxation, redistribution, and social welfare would imply a major transfer of sovereignty from member states to Brussels. Will member states agree to that? The German Constitutional Court has already ruled that the decision on revenue and expenditure of the public sector must remain in the hands of the Bundestag.

This leads to another important observation: an EU in charge of such major economic policies would need to have stronger democratic legitimacy. As the famous saying dating back to the American War of Independence goes: 'no taxation without representation.' Can the EU offer such representation? So far, we have pretty opaque parliamentary representation in Europe, which struggles to be recognized by Europe's citizens. Although the European Parliament acquired ever more powers, fewer and fewer people bothered to vote in successive European elections. These elections usually served as popularity contests for the ruling national governments. They are hardly ever about European matters and they do not define the future European government. The European Parliament does not have a governing cabinet or a governing programme to sustain or oppose. Despite changes introduced in the Lisbon Treaty, the Parliament, the Commission, and the Council are still relatively independent. Cleavages within the European Parliament still break along national lines and not just along party affiliations as is sometimes alleged.[10]

Let's put it bluntly: the creation of a European federation would amount to the collective suicide of the member states. Why would they commit such an act? After all, they are masters of the EU as it is currently constructed. I therefore fully agree with Sergio Fabbrini's assertion that 'The EU can never become a full-scale parliamentary federal state, such as to reabsorb internally the member states and transform them into *Laender* as in the German experience. The nation-states cannot be abolished with the stroke of a pen.'[11]

The muddling-through alternative of benign neglect amounts to suicide too, but spread over time and thus appearing less dramatic. Under this scenario, the EU is being sacrificed in the hope that nation-states can survive and cooperate in a looser fashion. Disintegration progresses in disguise and sometimes in default. Europe's leaders do the minimum to avert a financial meltdown and political confrontation, but they do not invest their careers and resources in reforms with highly uncertain outcomes. They meet on a regular basis, smile in group photos, and send around reassuring tweets, but their policies amount to a public relations exercise with no effort to steer the EU into safe waters. In today's huge and multi-layered Union, bold reforms are contentious while timid ones are useless. Does anybody believe that a President of the European Commission elected by a popular vote will be able to bridge differences between creditor and debtor states within the EU? Would people treat the European Parliament more seriously if it no longer travelled between Strasbourg and Brussels?

There was always a temptation for like-minded and like-looking states to form a tightly integrated core, but it was never clear who would form such a core, which fields it ought to cover, and how far integration within the core should go. If France and Germany cannot agree on some basic issues, how likely is it that an agreement could be reached between several more states? And there would always be states worried about being excluded from the core while others would fear that joining the core would subject them to domination by other core members. These are questions that now besiege President Macron after his call for a leaner and tighter EU faced a wall of resistance from numerous states, including Germany.

Given all these complications, changing little or nothing may sound like a rational proposition. The problem is that muddling through does not solve the problems confronting Europe; moreover, it provides a breeding ground for counter-revolutionary politicians. The financial crisis of 2008 and the 2015 refugee crisis have exposed the weakness of Europe's institutions, divisions between member states, and limited public support for European endeavours. What looked to be a straightforward financial and migratory challenge became a social, political, cultural, and even ideological one. Suddenly under fire was not just a certain treaty or leadership position; at stake now is the future of the integration project together with its liberal foundations. The European Union is still alive, but it is difficult to hide that it does not function properly. The counter-revolutionary forces are ruthlessly exploiting the EU's vulnerability, as manifested by the Brexit referendum and its aftermath.

The Brexit Predicament

Brexit reveals numerous traps and flaws of European politics. It shows how difficult it is to make crucial European decisions involving the public. It illustrates how hard it is to negotiate relations between states within the EU. It proves that anti-Europeanism is paving the way for the rise of illiberal politics. Above all, Brexit demonstrates that the EU is no longer able to turn crises to its advantage. I expect both the UK and the EU will be weaker after completion of Brexit. In fact, I would not be surprised if both these unions disintegrate as a result of Brexit.

Democracy in Europe is said to be representative rather than plebiscitarian. Referenda are used seldom by nation-states with the exception of countries such as Switzerland. I explained the reason for this earlier: a referendum is a conflict-generating mechanism because the winner takes all and there is no incentive to compromise. A referendum rewards demagoguery, hype, and spin, and generates accidental rather than fair and effective outcomes. The problem is that the system of parliamentary representation within the EU is opaque and therefore governments often reach out to referenda to legitimate their policies regarding the EU. (In countries such as Denmark or

Ireland this is even legally required.) Since voters have generally little impact on European policies a referendum is often treated by them as a means to reflect their frustration. This is probably why the outcome of a referendum can never be taken for granted. One thing is certain, but seldom appreciated: the results of the European referenda always impact not only the country holding a referendum, but also other European states and their public who obviously could not take part in a referendum held in another country.

There are strong reasons to believe that David Cameron called the Brexit referendum to consolidate his position within the Tory party and he did not expect to lose. This is surprising given the way, in the past, Europe-related referenda went in such states as Ireland, Denmark, the Netherlands, and France. His negotiations with the EU in the months preceding the referendum also demonstrated that he was more interested in appeasing Tory backbenchers than in improving the EU or the British position within it.

The campaigns of the 'remain' and 'leave' camps were long and agonizing. Misinformation, smear, and spin intensified over time. This obviously rewarded the 'leave' camp which had few substantive arguments on its side and appealed to emotions, sometimes ugly ones as far as migrants are concerned. The 'remain' camp could hardly make the EU look better than it is and so it increasingly engaged in scaremongering. This did not go down well with the 'proud' British public. I do not think that many Britons cultivate nostalgia for imperial glory, but this does not mean that they support the kind of liberal regionalism embodied by the EU.

In the end symbolism prevailed over realism. The usually pragmatic Brits decided to embark on a road into the unknown. David Cameron lost not only the referendum, but also his job. Great Britain is now divided more than ever along political, regional, and generational lines. Some 64 per cent of over-65s voted for Brexit, while 71 per cent of under-25s voted to remain.[12] Scotland voted in favour of the UK staying in the EU by 62 per cent to 38 per cent—with all thirty-two council areas backing Remain.[13]

Eurosceptic fundamentalists have begun to dominate the ruling Tory party, yet their policies are poorly informed, contradictory, and not properly discussed even within Parliament. Supporters of Brexit promised to bring power back from Brussels to Westminster, but since the referendum they have tried to deprive Westminster of any meaningful say on the outcome of Brexit negotiations. Given the complex and secret nature of these negotiations citizens are not going to have much insight, let alone say, on what will be discussed and decided. So much for referenda empowering the people.

The situation does not look better on the other side of the English Channel. In Brussels no one is taking responsibility for the mess that is being created. Nobody answers the question 'who lost one of the most important EU member states?' European leaders simply blame the perfidious Albion, but as the famous saying goes, you need two to tango. The idea that punishing the UK will deter other states from leaving the Union is dangerous. The more citizens feel bullied by the EU, the more they rebel. Besides, 'punishing' the UK is going to harm numerous firms and consumers across the EU, not just across the UK. This is the logic of interdependence after all.

For a considerable period of time Europe will be focused on Brexit negotiations, neglecting many other crucial issues. This is because these negotiations are doomed to be cumbersome. It is not easy to untangle twenty thousand laws and regulations of the European *acquis*; there are numerous veto players on both sides of the negotiating table; and under the glare of the media emotions will play a greater role than rational calculations in the process of bargaining. 'Britain must embrace its new, nasty brand' in the Brexit negotiations, urged Tim Stanley in the *Daily Telegraph*. 'We want the world to love us for our tea and decency. But on this occasion we're going to have to fight—and if that means acting nasty to convince as nasty, so be it.'[14]

This time Uncle Sam won't be there to bring us all to our senses; Uncle Trump is likely to add to our complications. Brexit will create new dividing lines within the EU; the UK is already trying to bribe Poland and Hungary to help its case. Brexit will also create new dividing lines within the United Kingdom; Scotland and Northern Ireland have high stakes in the outcome of Brexit negotiations. Divisions within the Tory party regarding Brexit were cited as one of the reasons for Theresa May to call snap elections in 2017, but the party seems more divided after the elections than before them and its Brexit policy seems to be in tatters.

The idea that Brexit may well be good for the EU is absurd. 'We would finally be able to create a truly European defence after Brexit,' whispered an Italian diplomat to me. But the EU has lost one of the two serious European armies. A new building in Brussels does not amount to European defence. Can Czech and Belgian soldiers form the core of a robust European army?

Nor can I see more stringent European regulation of the financial sector after neo-liberal Britain leaves the single market. Numerous European governments are trying to charm London-based billionaires to move to their countries by offering tax exemptions. This will be an economic race to the bottom, not to the top. We will see more tax loopholes and protectionism on the one hand, and bankruptcies as well as precariat on the other. As always, the burden will not be distributed equally, creating further conflicts within and across individual states. This will only fuel nationalism across the continent. Since nation-states can no longer control economic flows, 'patriots' will concentrate on rewriting national histories, parading under national flags, and sponsoring national culture. Some of this can already be detected in the United Kingdom. As Philip Collins cynically observed in *The Times*: 'British politics after the EU referendum has descended into the vale of ignorance. Shared values with the Philippines, the colour of passports, the spirit of Elizabeth I at Tilbury addressing the troops gathered to push back the Armada as we contemplate a war with Spain over Gibraltar.'[15] According to YouGov data prepared for *The Independent*, 53 per cent of Leave voters want the death penalty brought back to the UK after Brexit, and 42 per cent of them want corporal punishment back in British schools.[16] I am not sure whether this resembles a tragedy or a farce, but I know that cleaning up the mess will take many years and perhaps tears.

Consolidation versus Reinvention

In most countries, the attack on European integration goes hand in hand with the attacks on liberal democracy and free trade, migration and a multi-cultural society, historical 'truths' and political correctness, moderate political parties and mainstream media, cultural tolerance and religious neutrality. In short, at stake is not just the future of the EU, but also the future of the liberal open society.

The counter-revolutionary forces are well organized, well financed, and ruthless in exploiting the EU's flaws. Yet, liberals cannot act as innocent victims of a malicious populist assault. The EU was an institution totally controlled by liberals and they are partly responsible for making the anti-European campaign relatively easy if not legitimate to some degree. Numerous pleas to reform the EU have been ignored even if coming from liberal intellectual circles. It has consistently been argued that the EU cannot assume ever more functions without offering adequate means of public representation and participation. Democracy and accountability could also be addressed by dispersing power to various regulatory agencies spread across the continent and away from the hierarchical centre in Brussels. None of these arguments have been taken on board by the EU.

The EU was also repeatedly warned that it is wrong to pretend that inter-country divisions are the only ones that really count, and that the choice is essentially between more or less Europe. Today, inequalities within states are the main cause of anti-Europeanism. Greeks or Italians may well complain about German rigidity, but their major source of frustration is stagnation, unemployment, and poverty.

Pleas to make the EU more flexible and diversified have also been ignored. Instead of concentrating on problem-solving capacities, the EU has been constructing the European centre of authority resembling a pyramid rather than concentric circles.

It has also been argued that for integration to be successful it needs to be carried out by multiple actors and not just by states. At the European decision-making table we find some 'failed' states such as Greece and some mini-states such as Latvia. Mega-cities generating most of Europe's innovation and growth such as London, Paris, Stockholm, Milan, Rotterdam, and Hamburg are denied direct access to European decision-making and resources.[17]

Obviously, fundamental reforms are always controversial, but they ought to be seriously considered and tried. The point is not to design a perfect European architecture, but to propose and undertake concrete steps for moving forward. We need to debate serious alternative visions of integration and see which ones can possibly work. We cannot just mimic reforms and pretend that the public is on our side. The President of the European Commission is proposing one plan after another without mastering adequate political support for his plans and backing them with adequate material resources. The President of the European Council is not even trying that. Most liberal politicians want simply to preserve what we already have against the assault of counter-revolutionary politicians. But the EU cannot be consolidated: it ought to be reinvented.

8

PEERING INTO THE FUTURE

These days one can make a fortune predicting the future. The ever-growing 'future industry' tells us who will win the next elections, which markets will generate profits, where terrorists will strike next, or when robots will take our jobs. We are bombarded with statistical 'evidence' confirming theories of doom and grandeur. We watch our academic colleagues and politicians playing the fortune-teller on our TV screens. Some go so far as to argue that 'the future has no future', while others invite us to consider what the world would be 'after the future'.[1] But as you know well, Ralf, in the business of predicting the future we hardly ever get value for money. Contemporary fortune-tellers may profit as never before, but they tend to be as wrong as those in the past. The Soviet system was said to be remarkably stable, and yet it collapsed with little advance notice, to the embarrassment of Western Kremlin watchers. The Habsburg Empire was said to be 'mad, bad and unfit to rule', and yet it persisted for over six hundred years.[2] Only a century or two from now, historians will tell us which facts and choices determined Europe's fortunes; of course provided that there will still be some historians in such a distant future. A group of fellow historians has recently been told by their university dean that history has no future and so the History Department is to be closed. All this does not mean that we can only pray and hope, but it does mean that our thoughts about the future are highly speculative and tainted by our personal experiences and prejudices. It looks as though Yogi Berra's famous saying still stands: 'It's tough to make predictions, especially about the future,' and notwithstanding all the scientific evidence.[3]

Moreover, the situation is not likely to be similar in all European countries. Liberals will hold on to power in some, while losing to the counter-revolutionary forces in others. Both winners and losers will have distinct local features: the economic situation in Austria is very different from that in Greece; the historical legacies of Portugal and Bulgaria are also as diverse as is their geopolitical situation. In other words, we can only be sure of one thing, namely, the future will be rather messy. This does not mean that Europe is doomed and there is no optimistic scenario to envisage. The irony of the current situation is that Europe is still a relatively wealthy, secure, educated, and organized part of the world. Most problems that Europe is facing at present are self-inflicted and can be remedied without any external, let alone heavenly, help. Let me therefore speculate what can be done and how.

A Sense of Direction

We may not know what the future will bring, but we can certainly know what kind of future we prefer and try to make it happen. Some people are happy to keep things as they are or want to push back the clock to a mythical past. This does not apply only in conservative circles. Many liberals long for the 'good old times' of the liberal reign and are unhappy to see any changes. I have in mind entrepreneurs cashing in on neo-liberal policies, journalists enjoying a monopoly on peoples' perceptions of the world, and politicians with access to lavish state resources. I have little in common with these groups of liberals. I do not even know whether they deserve to be called liberals.

On the other side, there are people busy inventing the future and chasing a Utopia. They are often guided by noble ideals, but they tend to be aggressive and dogmatic. I sympathize with Oscar Wilde's reflection that a world that does not include Utopia is not worth glancing at. Various Utopias made human progress possible; however, some kinds of Utopia seem to be from 'another universe'.[4] Moreover, radical thinkers often argue that means justify ends, and change ought to be revolutionary. The history of communism represents a good example of a mismatch between dream and reality. In fact, throughout modern history, imposing highly ambitious visions at the point of a bayonet has never worked in tandem with these proclaimed ambitions. This does not vindicate conservatism, but it begs for a different approach to change and progress.

This is why I am attracted to liberal ideas spelled out by a group of intellectuals born in my native part of Europe between Hanover, Vienna, and Riga. I have in mind Hannah Arendt, Isaiah Berlin, and Karl Popper. These quintessential liberals invited us to strive for an 'open society', to use the term coined by Popper, but keeping in mind that the process of arriving at the destination is as important as the final product.[5] They were critical of both revolution and counter-revolution; they wanted to move forward through reasoning, deliberation, and bargaining, not by using force. As you, Ralf, described your intellectual liberal hero: 'Popper is a radical defender of liberty, of change without bloodshed, of trial and error, and also of an active march towards the unknown, and thus of people who try to design their destiny.'[6] This is not much to hold onto for us contemporary liberals, but it is better than embarking on misguided Utopian projects or doing nothing.

We can surely agree that the march towards the future ought to be guided by norms and values. Principal liberal values such as individual liberty and equality, tolerance and anti-racism, the rule of law and accountable power, fair trade and diplomatic multilateralism have not lost their relevance despite all the problems described in this letter. They may be easier to preach than to realize, but there is no reason to believe that the counter-revolutionary insurgents can secure progress, individual well-being, and the general interest by questioning these values. Citizens should be free to pursue their happiness, to choose their religion or sexual orientation, to search for knowledge and to disseminate this knowledge.

This liberal creed is worth fighting for, but not in a crude and stubborn manner. Liberals must acknowledge that their values are rivalrous to some extent and perhaps even incommensurable. This has been explained most eloquently by Isaiah Berlin.[7] For instance, liberty and equality are both recognized as important liberal goods, even though they often collide in practice. Moreover, each of these goods or values is inherently pluralistic: there is a positive and negative liberty, and each of them is complex. Is freedom of information or the right to privacy more important? Different cultural forms will also generate different values with distinct features. Berlin made it clear that all these complications imply neither relativism nor nihilism, but he tried to warn us against simplistic assumptions and blind optimism.

Some choices ought to be made, however. Over the past three decades those who called themselves liberals have given priority to freedom over equality; economic goods received more attention (and protection) than political ones; private values have been cherished more than public values. These priorities need to be revisited. Rampant inequalities have made a mockery of liberty for large segments of European societies. We stopped questioning the political (and moral) implications of economic policies aimed at ever greater growth, competitiveness, and productivity. The cult of privatization has made states and individuals immune to the plea of those disadvantaged within our societies. Without redressing the normative agenda, the future of liberalism looks grim, in my view.

Open Society for the Twenty-First Century

For Karl Popper society is open when it 'sets free the critical powers of man', and he contrasted it with the 'closed' or 'tribal' society with its 'submission to magical forces'.[8] The open society was for Popper a form of social life and the values that are traditionally cherished in that social life such as freedom, tolerance, and justice. Democracy understood as a set of institutions was for him a different, albeit related matter. He expected the government to be responsive and tolerant in the open society, and political mechanisms to be flexible and transparent.

Popper wrote his famous book during the Second World War, but I agree with you, Ralf, that his ideas are anything but outdated. However, we should reckon with Zygmunt Bauman's warning that the 'openness' of the open society 'has acquired a new gloss, undreamt of by Karl Popper'.[9] Openness is not only about admitting its own imperfection and 'incompleteness'; it now also means 'a society impotent, as never before, to decide its own course with any degree of certainty, and to protect the chosen itinerary once it has been selected'.[10] By this Bauman chiefly means side-effects of 'selective globalization of trade and capital, surveillance and information, violence and weapons, crime and terrorism, all unanimous in their disdain of the principle of territorial sovereignty and their lack of respect for any state boundary'.[11]

Bauman does not recommend reinforcement or restoration of a state's borders. He simply warns that internationalization of economic transactions, communication flows, migratory movements, and regulatory regimes are now an inherent part of daily life. States may try to arrest globalization, and they may attempt to harden their borders in particular, but I believe that such efforts can be only partly successful, and they are likely to generate perverse results. Identity-based calls for hardening borders are exploiting or even stimulating racial and religious prejudices. It is virtually impossible to combat migration without damaging certain vital sectors of the economy. Giving preferential treatment to national economic champions may benefit certain firms, but not necessarily the population as such. Protectionism often leads to trade wars, not to mention that it rewards uncompetitive industries and causes job outsourcing. This is not an endorsement of a borderless Europe leading to chaos and anarchy, but an invitation to reconsider the relationship between territory, authority, and rights in Europe. We need to accept that in the modern world nation-states have lost or given up their power to control various kinds of economic, cultural, and even military borders, which means that we must think about sovereignty and social contracts in a novel way. National politicians may campaign under banners promising 'British jobs for

British workers' or 'France first', but in a highly interdependent and interconnected European environment these are empty and even dangerous slogans.

I therefore believe that nation-states should no longer dictate the rules of European politics; cities, regions, and transnational organizations should gain greater access to the European decision-making system and resources. For a few initial decades after the Second World War, European states could legitimate their extensive powers by claiming that they were the only providers of defence, democracy, and welfare. At present, these and other public goods are being offered by a variety of public and private actors, some local and some transnational. The digital revolution has also generated major transformations in production, communication, and security. Actors such as mega-cities have performed much better than states in this new digital environment, generating innovation and growth, but also experimenting with new forms of local democracy.[12] Responsibility for defence and security is shared by states, international institutions, and local police units, usually concentrated in large cities. Governance should reflect this new plurality. Of course, states are still important actors and I recognize the danger of creating various 'authority holes' leaving certain firms and citizens without jurisdiction and protection. Yet the counter-revolutionary effort to put nation-states back at the centre of economics and politics is futile and perhaps counter-productive. It is also illiberal because it builds walls separating businesses and people, discriminates against foreigners, and dismantles international institutions.

Of course, there is no need to embrace an all-or-nothing rationale; borders can be open or closed to various degrees. Liberals cannot forge their own vision of borders by decree; they need to negotiate with their voters the forms and scale of migration and trade. Sovereignty is also a matter of degree. Is Greece or Cyprus sovereign at present? If not, who exercises sovereignty on their behalf? Clearly, we need to sort these things out in an open and, it is hoped, consensual manner. Transnational politics and economics may well be the liberals' favourite, but they require viable transnational authorities. The only serious embodiment of such a transnational authority—the EU—is in the process of disintegration at present. Nation-states may well perform better when forming networks with European regions, cities, NGOs, and firms. However, networks ought to be accountable and transparent. They cannot act as 'floating islands' (*îles flottantes*) operating above the law and free from any coordination and supervision. Striving for an open society in this multi-level, plurilateral, cloudy, and at times chaotic European environment is anything but easy, but benign neglect will lead to ever greater counter-revolutionary advances. Anti-liberal insurgents are preying on our lack of imagination, involvement, and steadfastness.

Imagination and Experimentation

How is a new vision of the open society to be created? My reply is unpretentious: don't settle for the status quo, but try to experiment. Don't simply oppose assaults on the liberal record, but listen to the critics and search for alternative ways of doing liberal politics. Try to respond to societal needs and expectations by moving forward rather than backwards. Liberalism should embrace human progress and sustainable development and not try to turn back the clock of history, be it in the field of technology, governance, society, or environment.

Liberals are now focused on fencing off the counter-revolutionary tide, and invest little time in reinventing the liberal project. This is a serious mistake. This letter has stressed time and again that liberalism has become a shallow ideology of power with fading magnetism for the electorate. Too many shady politicians have joined the liberal project, perverted its ideals, and stained its image. Rule dressed as liberal has made many citizens impoverished and insecure; they are not likely to be content with the messages: no attractive alternatives to liberal Europe can possibly be conceived; there is no plan B; those who contemplate plan B are dangerous; and what is needed is resilience and restitution.

A festival of liberal ideas should take place across Europe. Liberals must rethink what they stand for and how they differ not only from anti-liberals, but also from each other. A cocktail of an accidental set of values, programmes, and policies united by the need to survive the counter-revolutionary offensive is a recipe for disaster. Pretending that this cocktail represents the only 'correct' liberal vision is false and politically damaging.

I strongly believe that the new version of the open society should take into account the plurality, heterogeneity, and hybridity of a Europe shaped by globalization, but I know that some of my liberal friends fear that this would lead to chaos, free riding, and conflict. I am in favour of embracing technological innovation and employing it for the service of the open society, but it is hard to deny that the internet is also being used as a tool of propaganda and repression. Machines will perform many jobs more cheaply and better than humans, but they may also leave many people with no prospect of employment. I look at migrants as a cultural and economic asset, but this does not mean that those who demand a set of stricter conditions for allowing migration are wrong. We need to debate all these complex, if not controversial, issues and search for practical solutions to them reflecting such core liberal values as openness and tolerance; individual rights and welfare; restraint, inclusiveness, and fairness.

Moving forward in an innovative manner requires more than dialogue and brainstorming; certain visions and programmes ought to be tried in practice. Some of them will succeed, while others will fail the test of reality and need to be replaced with different options. Let me repeat you, Ralf: liberalism represents an active march towards the unknown through trial and error. Liberalism should be neither about defending the status quo nor about imposing any dogma.

The most difficult task is to reinvent capitalism. I do not have sufficient economic expertise to propose such a reinvention plan, and to be honest, I am puzzled by some of the current economic discussions. I rather tend to agree with Kate Raworth's radical thesis that most economic theories are centuries out of date and unsuited for tackling the twenty-first century's challenges of climate change, poverty, and inequality.[13] These days, mainstream economists are more interested in abstract statistical modelling than in moral and philosophical facets of economic transactions. They tend to debate technical aspects of trade or monetary policy with no ambition to propose a new comprehensive system of political economy. In other words, we lack contemporary equivalents of Adam Smith, a father of liberal economics (although Amartya Sen, Dani Rodrik, and Joseph Stiglitz come close to this ideal).

Can anything meaningful be accomplished in the short to medium term? I obviously do not propose storming the modern equivalents of the Winter Palace, be it Canary Wharf in London or *La Défense* in Paris.[14] But equally I do not want to wait for capitalism to collapse due to its internal contradictions. I want to urge liberals to stop, if not reverse, the neo-liberal policies of deregulation and privatization. Those with money (often virtual money) should not feel free to abuse workers, damage the environment, and appropriate common cultural heritage. They should be adequately taxed and made account-able for breaking laws and regulations. Companies should be asked to have representatives of workers and consumers on their boards. The universal minimum wage should be tried less timidly.

Balancing the quest for corporate efficiency and social justice seems to me essential. In recent years, liberals have emphasized the former at the expense of the latter. They need to redress their priorities and adjust them to digitalized transnational markets, especially financial ones. The Tobin tax of financial transactions is one of those proposals that ought to be tried together with various forms of parallel curren-cies and 'timebanks'. We should also encourage various forms of shared economy. I am perfectly aware that TaskRabbit or Zipcar will not heal capitalism, but the point is to encourage experiments that will get us out of the current neo-liberal predicament. As Paul Mason rightly argued: 'Today the terrain of capitalism has changed: it is global, fragmentary, geared to small-scale choices, temporary work and multiple skill-sets.'[15] Capitalism of that sort needs to be tackled by concerted efforts from the bottom and the top, by a cocktail of incentives and sanctions; by 'precision bombing' of such pathologies as tax havens or the precariat, but also by 'diplomacy' bringing together employers and employees, producers and consumers, bankers and their clients.

All these policies need to be introduced on a transnational basis and we need to experiment with different forms of transnational economic regulation; relying on the current dysfunctional EU is not sufficient. We need a polyphonic Europe with a variety of functional integrative networks organized horizontally rather than vertically.[16] The current emphasis on territorial rather than functional governance lumps together states regardless of their actual needs and situations; it creates an artificial border of Europe with privileged insiders, and outsiders who are discriminated against. It makes it difficult for non-territorial actors to join the integration project. In reality, different tasks concern a different territory as well as actors and therefore require diversified spatial and institutional arrangements. The point is not only that maritime traffic, for instance, concerns some states, regions, and cities more than others. The capacity of these public actors differs from field to field and from place to place. Compare tax collection capacity in Sweden and Bulgaria or in northern and southern Italy.

Beyond Parliamentary Representation

New thinking is especially needed in the field of democracy. Contemporary liberal politicians are averse to any meaningful experimentation, but the system of parliamentary representation is in deep trouble and we need to search for complementary or even alternative solutions. I lost any trust in the European Parliament after it chose Antonio Tajani as its President in early 2017. Mr Tajani is a close buddy of Silvio Berlusconi, helping him to get into power in the 1990s and then serving as his spokesmen justifying numerous indignities. Corruption and sex scandals have eventually caught up with Mr Berlusconi, but now Mr Tajani is (mis)using his position in Brussels to orchestrate Berlusconi's come back to the Italian (and European) corridors of power.

As explained earlier, the system of representation embodied by the European Parliament is opaque, probably beyond repair. The EP should therefore be allowed to do what it does best, a kind of auditing and monitoring of European institutions with no pretensions to act as a sovereign pan-European representative assembly.

While I have given up hopes of meaningful improvements of the pan-European system of representation, I still believe that national parliaments can be reformed. Parliaments can make their composition more representative in terms of electoral opinion and the voters' social composition. They can improve communication with their electorates. They can allow large groups of citizens to initiate bills.[17]

Reforms of parliaments will not produce wonders, however, and therefore we must try to build democracy on other pillars than representation: participation, deliberation, and contestation, most notably. As Nadia Urbinati convincingly argued, we should not assume that democracy is chiefly about representation: 'Democracy is a Greek word with no Latin equivalent', while representation is a 'Latin word with no Greek equivalent'.[18] The fusion between democracy and representation is thus a historical phenomenon that may not last forever.

Participation is chiefly about localism; the larger the unit the more difficult it is to offer citizens valuable forms of participation. The decision centre is further away in a larger unit and the power of a single vote is smaller with the increase in the size of the electorate. This has been argued by successive generations of political theorists from Jean Jacques Rousseau, to Immanuel Kant and Robert Dahl, and yet local democracy is still underestimated and underdeveloped. Most of the recent reforms aimed at devolution and decentralization empowered local elites rather than local citizens. This is chiefly because these reforms were organized by top party echelons and not by grass-root movements. I am more impressed by genuine local initiatives such as the Barcelona-style *municipalismo*. In fact, numerous European cities have already begun experimenting with novel forms of local democracy and we should study and encourage the most successful among them. As Giovanni Sartori put it forcefully: 'real democracy can only be, and must be, participatory democracy.'[19]

Deliberation is increasingly about e-democracy. Digital technology has offered novel ways not only of deliberation, but also of participation in public affairs and scrutiny of officials. The internet can narrow space between the government and the people; it can transcend borders with remarkable ease. The notion of a cosmopolitan democracy would be a pure fantasy without the internet. Digital communication technologies have enabled a variety of local political actors to enter international arenas once exclusive to national states. Thanks to the internet even those who are geographically immobile can become part of global or regional politics. NGOs, indigenous peoples, immigrants, and refugees can now make claims on states and international bodies or practice oppositional politics. All this has been vividly illustrated by Saskia Sassen.[20]

The overall conclusion from this analysis is simple: the internet has changed the meaning of democracy in the same way the invention of print did. It is enough to have a quick glance on Facebook or Twitter to see the formerly unknown scale of citizenry debating public affairs. Some of these exchanges are not necessarily a model of enlightened dialogue; yet, scrutinizing and criticizing the government is the daily bread of democracy. The internet has also led to more institutional forms of deliberation and monitoring: online surveys and petitions, focus groups, civic dialogues, open social forums, peer-to-peer networks, deliberative polling, crowdsourcing, online chat and group decision-making, digital advocacy services, e-learning, and e-participation have blossomed in recent years.

In your time, Ralf, nobody talked about 'wiki-democracy' (creating a 'shadow' government programme on a wiki by various social networks) or about 'Delphi method' (combining the open communication of self-organized virtual communities with the structured communication of closed panels, including members of the policy-community). Today, these digital initiatives with fancy names put politicians, parties, and elected governments permanently 'on their toes', to use John Keane's expression.[21] They question the authority of formal institutions, force politicians to change their agendas, and break long-standing corporatist arrangements. According to Keane, democracy is about self-governed networks monitoring traditional political institutions and forcing them to make regular adjustments of their policies. Democracy is no longer about delegating power to elected officials within confined territorial states. Nor is democracy a government implementing the common 'will' of any given (national) majority.

I am not sure that all this is necessarily good news. Access to social networks can be restricted for various formal and informal reasons such as class, profession, or money. The notion of public participation within the prime monitoring institution, the media, is very one-sided: audiences are invited to take part in media debates, but editors can choose that only some of the inputs reach the public. Networks may well be self-governed, but they are not always governed in a demo-cratic manner, and they are notoriously unaccountable. Monitoring democracy tends to focus on single simple issues better than on complex aggregated problems requiring broader, informed, and sus-tained deliberation. The selection of issues highlighted by monitoring institutions can be either manipulated or accidental. For instance, the public's attention is often diverted to politicians' private lives and away from their voting records. All this does not mean that liberals should dismiss new technologies as a means of improving democracy. The point is to make the dense web of digital networks more transparent, accountable, and responsive to people's quest for freedom and equal-ity. The point is to utilize the internet in the service of democracy. So far, remarkably little has been done in this direction. As Stephen Coleman observed, the internet transformed a range of social relation-ships but 'democratic governance is an exception to those transform-ations. There has been no shortage of e-rhetoric from governments at all levels (local, national, and transnational), but in practice an ethos of centralized institutionalism has prevailed.'[22]

Contestation is also an important, but under-utilized democratic pillar. This is surprising given that there was always a vocal group of democratic theorists arguing that the sovereignty of people lies not so much in electoral authorization as in the right of resistance.[23] Contestation can be political and juridical. The former is spontaneous and often chaotic, while the latter is institutionalized and structured. The former takes place not only on the streets and within industrial plants, but also on the web. Cyber disobedience and 'hactivism' are increasingly in vogue, but with mixed results. Juridical contestation, on the other hand, takes place in parliaments and courts. Citizens are being given legal opportunities to contest the decisions they find unjust or harmful to their interests. They can do it directly through private litigation in courts or indirectly through the office of Ombudsman. The powers and resources of Ombudsmen can be beefed up significantly. Citizens can be given more rights to sue their governments in national and international courts. Juridical contestation is usually more deliberative, inclusive, and responsive than political contestation and it should therefore be encouraged before things get out of hand on the streets and in industrial plants.

Strategy and Agency

Liberals, like all groups in society, contain optimists and fatalists. Optimists predict the counter-revolutionary forces will discredit themselves within the next three to four years, the grass-root pressure should intensify in this period, and restoration of the liberal reign will then be completed across Europe at the same time President Trump is being removed from the White House after his first 'disastrous' term in office. I fear this scenario is too good to be true. In my view, the counter-revolutionary upsurge will last longer than four years, and there is no guarantee that liberals will return to power after the fall of the counter-revolutionary forces.

Fatalists fear that anti-liberals will not be defeated at the ballot box. In their view, counter-revolutionaries will brainwash the electorate and seduce it with fairy-tale promises. When in power, anti-liberals are not likely to allow fully free elections anyway. They should therefore be overthrown by a wave of mass public protests, perhaps even by force. 'They are applying the vast state machine of repression and propaganda against us'—a Polish female liberal has told me—'and we can hardly defend our liberal cause with bare hands.' I have heard similar comments from a frustrated Greek critic of Syriza.

My own take on the future is somewhere between these two extreme positions. The counter-revolution will not be defeated by rational persuasion alone. Numerous forms of civic mobilization would have to be employed in defence of liberal values and institutions, although I would urge my liberal friends to resist any temptation to use violence, even when confronted with violence. The history of civic resistance from Mahatma Ghandi to Martin Luther King, Vaclav Havel, and Lech Walesa has shown the effectiveness of non-violent struggle. Using violence for political ends is not only illiberal, but it is also self-defeating. Right-wing nationalists are likely to mobilize more people accustomed to using sticks and Molotov cocktails than liberals are.

Civic mobilization is important, but it is not sufficient. Liberals will not win back disenchanted voters by marching with banners offering more of the same. They need to propose new visions of democracy, capitalism, and integration, which is anything but easy. It would probably take several years for sociologists, economists, and philosophers to spell out such a vision. It would then take another year or two for the media (new and old) to translate this vision into a 'user friendly' language. Only by then would some gifted liberal politicians be able to put on their banners the essence of this vision and hopefully get the majority of people behind them. In short, we are talking about fifteen years of climbing the 'valley of tears', to use your own expression, Ralf.

Liberal political activists and their media seem currently obsessed with the question of leadership. Will Angela Merkel save liberal Europe? Is Matteo Renzi or Emmanuel Macron the right person to lead centre-left liberals? If my schedule of a liberal comeback is correct, the issue of leadership will become crucial more than a decade from now, not earlier. This does not mean that in the meantime the leadership question is irrelevant. Obviously, those who betrayed liberal ideals should not be put in charge of the liberal renewal. The liberal record of Merkel or Renzi is anything but straightforward, while Macron still has to prove his liberal credentials. Yet, I should quickly add that clueless and uncharismatic leaders are not going to do any good either. The same applies to charismatic leaders with silly ideas. In other words, we need a sense of direction before we choose leaders. The greatest quality of a leader is to serve the community of people sharing certain values. What kind of community can liberals lead to this better future? Which groups will possibly unite behind the renewed liberal programme? Who will the social agents of change be?

Paul Mason believes that modern capitalism has united many diverse groups: 'By creating millions of networked people, financially exploited but with the whole of human intelligence one thumb-swipe away, info-capitalism has created a new agent of change in history: the educated and connected human being.'[24] This may be over-optimistic, but there is no reason to embrace the opposite view which only sees atomized individuals living in a small digital bubble of the 'Daily Me'.[25] The internet has certainly empowered the individual, but it has not killed the notion of society. By changing the pattern of social interaction, the internet has created a new form of society: the network society (to use Manuel Castells's term).[26]

The network society is pluralistic and at times chaotic, but it is neither passive nor purposeless. In fact, recent studies of collective action have shown the remarkable power of social media to mobilize wide strata of society for purposeful political change. Causes of social mobilization differ from place to place. The motivation of various groups interested in change is anything but coherent. Those campaigning for gay rights, for instance, have a different agenda from those campaigning for the minimum wage. They may unite against a major internal or external danger, but they are not necessarily bound by a common work experience, race, religion, and social status. The challenge for liberals is to attract those various segments of the network society and make them press for liberal change.

You would notice, Ralf, that I am not referring to traditional social classes or political parties. I simply think that they are no longer vital bodies able to move things forward. The working class has become diversified, de-unionized, and detached from concerns of those in the greatest need such as the masses of unemployed youth, or migrants. Political parties have lost touch with ordinary citizens; they are merely devices for competing elites to win elections. This does not mean that there are no specific problems related to the traditional manual working class employed in the dying industries, and I am certainly not prepared to see the working class as 'Thick. Violent. Criminal.'[27] Nor do I think that trade unions are a relic of the past. Yet, it is hard to deny that in the current highly automated and digitalized European economies the notion and role of the working class is different from the one you, Ralf, analysed in the late 1950s.[28] A similar comment can be made about political parties.

The counter-revolutionary forces pit 'ordinary people' against 'the elite'; the liberal forces must show that the elites and the people can work together for common causes. In fact, liberals need to be able to show that diversified groups at various levels of society are able to engage in dialogue and negotiation, leading to compromises.

Compromise between diverse groups is easier when none of them insist on certain dogmas. Diverse groups should have a common sense of direction, but the inclusive process of change (and not just the desired product) is the key to forming coalitions. Aversion to radical politics is also likely to make dialogue easier. This is how the Spanish diversified opposition to the Franco regime forged a Mancloa Pact in 1977. This is how the internally conflicted anti-communist forces sat with the internally conflicted communist forces at the Polish

Round Table of 1989. In both cases the liberal manual of politics led to a pact among people competing for power and resources. The alternative scenario implies a victory by a single doctrinaire force imposing its own utopia on the entire polity.

The New Beginning

Dear Ralf, it is time to bring this long letter to a close. Unlike you, three decades earlier, I am not in danger of finishing this letter on a lyrical note. I am disappointed, if not angry, that liberal ideals have been compromised or betrayed by the post-1989 generation of politicians and intellectuals across Europe. The counter-revolution will not just stop at correcting liberals' mistakes; it will go further by destroying many institutions without which democracy cannot function and capitalism becomes predatory. As a boy in communist Poland I dreamt about a Europe without walls and oppressive governments. I thought that the ideal of freedom could make life better not just for those living behind the Iron Curtain, but also for those living in poor suburbs of London, Paris, and Madrid. I hoped that liberal politicians would not only make us more affluent, but also more safe. This dream has now been crushed. I expect life to be much harder in the coming years before it becomes any better. It did not have to be that way.

You may ask, Ralf, why I am pointing fingers at our fellow liberals, and not at counter-revolutionary forces. Am I not legitimizing the anti-liberal turn? Am I not applying different normative standards to the liberals and to their opponents? These are fair questions. There are numerous critical works analysing the anti-liberal surge, and I preferred to write on the topic less covered. I also think that without a serious discussion of what went wrong with the liberal project it would be difficult for liberals to come back and defeat the anti-liberal temptation. And yes, it is true that I have higher expectations from the liberals than from the enemies of the open society. I was one of those who believed that liberals would make Europe a better place; I do not have similar expectations from the counter-revolutionary forces. In fact, I fear that they will make Europe a pretty inefficient and perhaps horrid place.

Despite all the gloom expressed on these pages I still believe in a happy ending. The happy ending does not mean the return of what we have had for the past three decades; it means correcting past mistakes and forging a renewed liberal agenda that is well suited for the Europe of the twenty-first century. Not only the programme but also the leadership should be changed. My generation should allow younger people to take control over their destiny. I trust not only their computer skills but also their sense of fairness and realism. Sadly, the latter seems in short supply among beneficiaries of the post-1989 liberal revolution.

Democracy is not safe when we question the wisdom of electoral choices. Equality is not served when we accuse poor people of being stupid and prone to manipulation. Liberty is not going to prevail in an atmosphere of hate and vengeance directed against political opponents. When I say these things I am reminded that Hitler was also elected. I am urged to name and resist the real evil. I am told that experts have more knowledge to cope with complex problems than those who are poor and thus undereducated. Needless to say, this is all true and can hardly be questioned. Yet, I believe that we do not need to behave like beasts in order to defeat beasts. I believe that all people, and not just a few, should be free and equal. I do not think that democracy is only about elections, but without elections we can hardly talk about democracy.

Like you, Ralf, I believe that the situation differs 'from place to place and from time to time'. We are both impatient with those who 'peddle patent medicines'. We both believe that liberty is a goal worth fighting for, although 'the path to it has many pitfalls'. We can help master some of them, with energy and purpose. 'The rest is luck,' however.[29]

I will not just 'keep my fingers crossed and hope for the best'.[30] I intend to travel and speak out across the old continent trying to alter the views of my fellow liberals. Many of them will not like to hear my message, but I am determined to follow your dictum spelled out as early as 1963: 'the fundamental responsibility of intellectuals is to doubt all received wisdom, to wonder what is taken for granted, to question all authority, and to pose all those questions that otherwise no-one else dares to ask.'[31]

Very sincerely yours,
Jan Zielonka
Oxford, October 2017

ENDNOTES

All web addresses were accessed in June 2017.

Prologue

1. Ralf Dahrendorf, *Reflections on the Revolution in Europe* (London: Times Books, 1990).
2. Edmund Burke wrote a letter intended to have been sent to a gentleman in Paris. See Edmund Burke, *Reflections on the Revolution in France*, ed. Frank M. Turner (New Haven: Yale University Press, 2003), originally published in 1790 in London by James Dodsley, Pall Mall.
3. See the obituary of Ralf Dahrendorf published in *The Guardian*, <www. theguardian.com/politics/2009/jun/19/ralf-dahrendorf-obituary-lords-lse>.
4. The description 'intellectual provocateur' appears in a review of my book in *Foreign Affairs*, <www.foreignaffairs.com/reviews/2014-08-18/eu-doomed>.

Chapter 1

1. Beppe Grillo, cited by *Today* on 20 June 2016, <www.today.it/politica/elezioni/grillo-raggi-appendino.html>.
2. Interview with Jarosław Kaczyński on 11 July 2016, <www.rp.pl/Prawo-i-Sprawiedliwosc/307109958-Kaczynski-Nie-jestem-dyktatorem.html#ap-2>.
3. In 2000 Mény and Surel have identified three political conditions behind the emergence of populism: 1. the crisis of the structures of political intermediation; 2. the personalization of political power; and 3. the increasing role of the media in political life. See Yves Mény and Yves Surel, *Par le peuple, pour le peuple* (Paris: Fayard, 2000), ch. 2.
4. Although in 2017 the Liberal ALDE group in the European Parliament counted no less than seven sitting prime ministers. See <www.aldegroup. eu/>.
5. According to Jacques Rupnik, 1989 'clearly represents a *caesura*, the closure of the "short twentieth century" (1914–1989), marked by two world wars and

two totalitarianisms that originated in Europe', Jacques Rupnik, *1989 as a Political World Event* (London: Routledge, 2013), 7.

6. Anti-establishment politicians and parties have operated in Europe for many years, but till recently the establishment was able to keep them under control in all European countries. Front National has gained 11.2 per cent of votes already in the 1984 European Parliament elections. New Democracy party has won 6.7 per cent of votes in the 1991 parliamentary elections in Sweden. The Freedom Party has won 26.9 per cent in the 1999 parliamentary elections in Austria. Pim Fortuyn's party has won 17 per cent in the 2002 parliamentary elections in Holland, only nine days after its leader had been assassinated by an animal rights activist. Jörg Heider's Freedom Party even entered the Austrian coalition government in 2000, but lost half of its previous share in the elections two years later. Jarosław Kaczyński's Law and Justice party formed a government in Poland in 2005 together with two smaller anti-establishment parties, Self-defence (left-wing) party and the League of Polish Families, but they were replaced in two years by a government formed by the parties of the establishment. No wonder Cas Mudde called these parties 'dogs that bark loudly but hardly ever bite'. See Cas Mudde (2013), 'Three Decades of Populist Radical Right Parties in Western Europe: So What?', *European Journal of Political Research*, 52/1 (2013), 1–19.

7. Robert A. Dahl, 'A Democratic Dilemma: System Effectiveness versus Citizens Participation', *Political Science Quarterly*, 109/1 (1994), 23–4.

8. Colin Crouch, *Post-Democracy* (Cambridge: Polity, 2004), and Paul Mason, *Post-capitalism: A Guide to our Future* (London: Allen Lane, 2015).

9. See an interview with a leading German sociologist, Ulrich Beck, on 25 March 2013, <www.socialeurope.eu/2013/03/germany-has-created-an-accidental-empire/>. Also Ulrich Beck, *German Europe* (Cambridge: Polity, 2013).

10. For instance, the Dutch MP Geert Wilders, from the Party of Freedom, encouraged his supporters to chant that they want 'fewer' Moroccans in the Netherlands and Lega Nord MEP Mario Borghezio described the Italian government as 'bongo bongo' after Cecile Kyenge became Italy's first black minister.

11. <www.theguardian.com/commentisfree/2017/mar/11/farage-assange-shameless-illiberal-alliance>.

12. Cas Mudde, 'The Populist Zeitgeist', *Government and Opposition*, 39/4 (2004), 543.

13. Margaret Canovan, 'Trust the People! Populism and the Two Faces of Democracy', *Political Studies*, 47/1 (1999), 12.

14. For an analysis of populist rhetoric see Toril Aalberg, Frank Esser, Carsten Reinemann, Jesper Stromback, and Claes De Vreese (eds.), *Populist Political Communication in Europe* (London: Routledge, 2017). See also <http://counter point.uk.com/wp-content/uploads/2015/01/Responding-to-Populist-Rhetoric-A-Guide.pdf>.

15. Jaroslava Barbieri told me in conversation that populists' activity reminded her of carnival as a festivity during the Middle Ages. It celebrated the obscene and everything that undermined the established order of things. It translated the divine, political, and moral order into grotesque expressions. Yet, while being openly celebrated for a brief period, this obscene element did not represent symbolically a made-up reality for the sake of mere entertainment. It was something deeply present in people's minds under the surface of the everyday convention regarding what the order of things should be. We may define populist leaders as clowns, and their statements as 'ridiculous', or 'absurd', but they actually do appeal to things or ideas that for some reason have not been suppressed by the dominant post-1989 order and discourse. We should keep in mind that the medieval carnival festivities were allowed by the authority of the Church only for a specific period of time.

16. <www.theguardian.com/commentisfree/2017/mar/30/britain-treaty-europe-dead-brexit-eu>.

17. <https://milanofinanza.it/news/fincantieri-ugl-macron-ha-dichiarato-guerra-a-principi-ue-201707281632149952 or <http://ilmessaggero.it/primopiano/esteri/scelta_parigi_colpita_nazionalizzata_emmanuel_macron-2588037.html>.

18. <www.nytimes.com/2017/01/24/world/europe/mark-rutte-netherlands-muslim-immigrants-trump.html>.

19. <https://www.theguardian.com/world/2017/mar/19/dutch-election-rutte-wilders-good-populism-bad->.

20. See a 2015 study of the Deutsche Bank, <www.dbresearch.com/PROD/DBR_INTERNET_EN-PROD/PROD0000000000354812/A_profile_of_Europe%E2%80%99s_populist_parties%3A_Structures.PDF>.

21. <www.bbc.com/news/world-europe-30318898>. Also <www.nybooks.com/daily/2015/10/14/orban-hungary-sorry-about-prime-minister/>.

22. According to Ivan Krastev, though, 'weak elite commitment to the values of liberal democracy' is less responsible for the rise of illiberalism than 'the failures of liberalism to deliver'. See Ivan Krastev, 'Liberalism's Failure to Deliver', *Journal of Democracy*, 4/27 (2016), 35–7.

23. This quote comes from a lecture given in August 1963 to the Indian Institute of Public Administration published in, among others, Karl Popper, *After the Open Society: Selected Social and Political Writings*, ed. Jeremy Shearmur and Piers Norris Turner (London: Routledge, 2012), 231.

Chapter 2

1. Michael Freeden, *Liberalism: A Very Short Introduction* (Oxford: Oxford University Press, 2015), 16.

2. Leszek Kołakowski, *Modernity on Endless Trial* (Chicago: University of Chicago Press, 1980), 225–7.

3. Martin Krygier, Review of Ben Golder, *Foucault and the Politics of Rights* (Stanford, CA: Stanford University Press, 2015), published in *Jotwell Jurisprudence* (forthcoming).

4. Martin Krygier, 'Conservative-Liberal-Socialism Revisited', *The Good Society*, 1/11 (2002), 6.

5. Ralf Dahrendorf, *Reflections on the Revolution in Europe* (London: Times Books, 1990), 25–6.

6. <www.theatlantic.com/magazine/archive/1997/02/the-capitalist-threat/376773/>.

7. Ernesto Laclau and Chantal Mouffe, *Hegemony and Socialist Strategy: Towards a Radical Democratic Politics* (London: Verso, 2001).

8. Thomas Piketty, *Capital in the Twenty-First Century* (Cambridge, MA: Belknap, 2014), 1.

9. <www.bild.de/politik/ausland/polen/hat-die-regierung-einen-vogel-44003034,var=a,view=conversionToLogin.bild.html>.

10. Tony Judt, *Thinking the Twentieth Century* (London: William Heinemann, 2012), 317.

11. <www.oxforddictionaries.com/press/news/2016/12/11/WOTY-16>.

12. <www.washingtonpost.com/news/the-fix/wp/2016/11/16/post-truth-named-2016-word-of-the-year-by-oxford-dictionaries/?utm_term= .4a37750de0be>.

13. William Davies, *The Happiness Industry: How the Government and Big Business Sold Us Well-being* (London: Verso, 2016).

14. <www.theguardian.com/politics/2016/jun/14/osborne-predicts-30bn-hole-in-public-finance-if-uk-votes-to-leave-eu>.

15. <https://theconversation.com/the-surprising-origins-of-post-truth-and-how-it-was-spawned-by-the-liberal-left-68929>.

16. <www.theguardian.com/world/2017/feb/05/marine-le-pen-promises-liberation-from-the-eu-with-france-first-policies>. Also <www.lemonde.fr/election-presidentielle-2017/article/2017/02/05/marine-le-pen-donne-rendez-vous-a-lyon-le-meme-jour-que-jean-luc-melenchon_5074887_4854003.html>.

17. See Michael Sandel, *Liberalism and the Limits of Justice* (Cambridge: Cambridge University Press, 1982); Charles Taylor, 'Cross Purposes: the Liberal-

Communitarian Debate', in Nancy Resenblum (ed.), *Liberalism and the Moral Life* (Cambridge, MA: Harvard University Press, 1989), 171–6; Philip Selznick, *The Moral Commonwealth: Social Theory and the Promise of Community* (Berkeley, CA: University of California Press, 1992); and Michael Walzer, 'Communitarian Critique of Liberalism', *Political Theory* 1990, 9–11.

18. Michael Freeden has pointed out that liberalism evolves differently not only over time but also across space. The civil society discourse is chiefly an east and central European discourse, notably anti-statist for obvious reasons relating to the communist experience. American political philosophers write about liberalism-communitarianism mainly in North American terms, and they often ignore or misread the history of European liberalism. According to Freeden, most (Western) European liberals have moved away from the 'atomistic' model of society with the ascendance of the welfare state, inspired by the work of 'social liberal' precursors such as Carlo Rosselli and Leonard T. Hobhouse. See Michael Freeden, 'European Liberalisms: An Essay in Comparative Political Thought', *European Journal of Political Theory*, 7/1 (2008), 9–30.

19. Stephen Holmes, *The Anatomy of Antiliberalism* (Cambridge, MA: Harvard University Press, 1993), 180.

20. This has not always been the case. Mazzini and Gladstone have been seen as representing a brand of liberal nationalism, for instance. For a comprehensive analysis of the relationship between liberalism and nationalism see Yael Tamir, *Liberal Nationalism* (Princeton: Princeton University Press, 1993).

21. Charles S. Maier, 'Territorialisten und Globalisten: die beiden neuen "Parteinen" in der heutigen Demokratie', *Transit*, 14 (Winter 1997), 5–14.

22. <www.vagalume.com.br/bob-dylan/what-good-am-i.html>. Copyright © 1989 by Special Rider Music. All rights reserved. International copyright secured. Reprinted by permission.

23. Philip Selznick, *The Moral Commonwealth: Social Theory and the Promise of Community* (Berkeley, CA: University of California Press, 1992); Philip Selznick, 'From Socialism to Communitarianism', in Michal Walzer (ed.), *Towards a Global Civil Society* (Oxford: Berghahn Books, 1995), 128.

24. Stefan Auer, *Liberal Nationalism in Central Europe* (London: Routledge, 2004); see also Stefan Auer, 'New Europe: Between Cosmopolitan Dreams and Nationalist Nightmares', *Journal of Common Market Studies*, 48/5 (2010), 1163–84.

25. Freeden, 'European Liberalisms', 14.

26. <www.newyorker.com/magazine/1967/02/25/truth-and-politics>.

Chapter 3

1. These quotes come from Dahrendorf's *Reflections on the Revolution in Europe*, cited in the Prologue. The distinction between liberal and egalitarian democracy comes from Dahrendorf's endorsement of Colin Crouch's book *Post-Democracy* (Cambridge: Polity, 2004).

2. <www.bing.com/search?q=Anocracy&filters=ufn%3a%22Anocracy%22+sid%3a%229bae7a5e-3eed-f28f-a63a-fee8b1709d66%22&FORM=SNAPST>.

3. See the Voter Turnout Database, <www.idea.int/data-tools/data/voter-turnout>; Ingrid van Biezen, Peter Mair, and Thomas Poguntke, 'Going, Going . . . Gone? The Decline of Party Membership in Contemporary Europe', *European Journal of Political Research*, 51/1 (2012), 24–56, and the Standard Eurobarometer, <http://ec.europa.eu/public_opinion/archives/eb/eb83/eb83_ first_en.pdf>.

4. Peter Mair, *Ruling the Void* (London: Verso, 2013), 1.

5. The average age of members of the UK Conservative Party is 68 (some statistics even put it at 74). This obviously begs the question 'who does this party represent?' See Brian Wheeler and Chris Davies, '"Swivel-Eyed Loons" or Voice of the People?', *BBC News*, 21 May 2013; available at: <www.bbc.com/news/uk-politics-22607108>. Also Ross Clark, 'End of the Party—How British Political Leaders Ran Out of Followers', *Spectator*, 14 September 2013, available at <www.spectator.co.uk/features/9019201/the-end-of-the-party/>. Remarkably, the Labour Party gathered numerous new and usually young members after Jeremy Corbyn assumed the leadership. The number of full members has moved from 190,000 in May 2015 to 515,000 in July 2016—an influx of 325,000 new members. For a comparative analysis of the old and new members and their background see <http://blogs.lse.ac.uk/europpblog/2016/11/25/>.

6. <www.buzzfeed.com/charliewarzel/trump-trolls-find-new-tactics-to-spread-false-voting-informa?utm_term=.ykELdz02l#.adNd9gr4Y>, or <www.buzzfeed.com/craigsilverman/how-macedonia-became-a-global-hub-for-pro-trump-misinfo?utm_term=.mfOAYMzb3#.wsXvO8oGV>.

7. Giandomenico Majone, 'Temporal Consistence and Policy Credibility: Why Democracies Need Non-Majoritarian Institutions', European University Institute, *RSC Working Paper*, 96/57, 12.

8. Alec Stone Sweet, *Governing with Judges* (Oxford: Oxford University Press, 2000), 105.

9. This *Daily Mail* headline appeared after the three High Court judges ruled that the Executive must consult Parliament before invoking Article 50 of the European Treaties following the results of the Brexit referendum.

10. <http://webarchive.nationalarchives.gov.uk/20140122145147/http:/www.levesoninquiry.org.uk/>.

11. Interview with Adam Michnik published online in October 2016 at <www.opinie.wp.pl/adam-michnik-polska-nie-zasłużyła-na-pis-6048429975437953a>.

12. <www.standard.co.uk/news/politics/robert-peston-attacks-brexit-campaign-for-mad-slur-over-tv-debate-with-pm-a3246361.html>.

13. Saskia Sassen, *Territory, Authority Rights: From Medieval to Global Assemblages* (Princeton: Princeton University Press, 2006).

14. Stephen Krasner, *Sovereignty, Organized Hypocrisy* (Princeton: Princeton University Press, 1999).

15. Wolfgang Merkel, 'The Challenge of Capitalism to Democracy. Reply to Colin Crouch and Wolfgang Streeck', *Zeitschrift für Vergleichende Politikwissenschaft*, 1/10 (2016), 78.

16. Ralf Dahrendorf, 'The Challenge For Democracy', *Journal of Democracy*, 14/4 (2003), 106, and Juan J. Linz and Alfred C. Stepan, *Problems of Democratic Transition and Consolidation: Southern Europe, South America, and Post-Communist Europe* (Baltimore: Johns Hopkins University Press, 1996), 16–10.

17. Constitutional patriotism is a noble idea, but it can hardly replace nationalism as a unifying political factor without a common history, culture, and, indeed, constitution. This has been acknowledged even by Jürgen Habermas in *Europe: The Faltering Project* (Cambridge: Polity, 2009), 79–88. See also Richard Bellamy, *Political Constitutionalism: A Republican Defence of the Constitutionality of Democracy* (Cambridge: Cambridge University Press, 2007), 6 and 235.

18. Jan-Werner Müller, 'The Promise of Demoi-cracy: Diversity and Domination in the European Public Order', in Jürgen Neyer and Antje Wiener, *The Political Theory of the European Union* (Oxford: Oxford University Press, 2010), 197–203.

19. Stein Rokkan et al., *Centre–Periphery Structures in Europe* (New York: Campus, 1987), 17–18.

20. Wolfgang Merkel, 'Is Capitalism Compatible with Democracy?' *Zeitschrift für Vergleichende Politikwissenschaft*, 2/8 (2014), 109.

21. Stefano Bartolini, *Restructuring Europe: Centre Formation, System Building and Political Structuring between the Nation-State and the European Union* (Oxford: Oxford University Press, 2005), p. xiv.

22. Daniele Archibugi, 'Cosmopolitan Democracy and its Critics. A Review', *European Journal of International Relations*, 10/3 (2004), 437–73.

23. Giovanni Sartori, *The Theory of Democracy Revisited*, Part One: *The Contemporary Debate* (Chatham, NJ: Chatham House, 1987), 115.

Chapter 4

1. Jeremy Rifkin, *The European Dream: How Europe's Vision of the Future Is Quietly Eclipsing the American Dream* (New York: Tarcher/Penguin, 2004). See also Mark Leonard, *Why Europe Will Run the 21st Century* (London: Harper Collins, 2005).

2. François Heisbourg, *La Fin du rêve européen* (Paris: Stock, 2013); Anthony Giddens, *Turbulent and Mighty Continent: What Future for Europe?* (Cambridge: Polity, 2013), and George Soros with Gregor Peter Schmitz, *The Tragedy of the European Union: Disintegration or Revival?* (New York: Public Affairs, 2014).

3. <www.financialsecrecyindex.com/index.php>, also <www.dw.de/the-whos-who-of-european-tax-havens/a-16753202>.

4. In 2015–17 growth has slightly picked up in Europe, but it remains to be seen whether this modest rise is sustainable. For optimistic forecasts see <https://ec.europa.eu/info/business-economy-euro/economic-performance-and-forecasts/economic-forecasts/winter-2017-economic-forecast_en>.

5. Helicopter money represents an unconventional tool of monetary policy that involves printing large sums of money and distributing it to the public in order to stimulate the economy. See e.g. <www.theguardian.com/business/ng-interactive/2015/apr/29/the-austerity-delusion>; see also Milton Friedman, *The Optimum Quantity of Money: And Other Essays* (Chicago: Aldine, 1969).

6. <www.tradingeconomics.com/euro-area/gdp-growth>.

7. <http://kulturaliberalna.pl/2015/06/30/polska-prekariat-definicja-standing-tyrowicz/>.

8. <http://ec.europa.eu/eurostat/documents/2995521/7766821/3-12122016-AP-EN.pdf/910ee81b-3d8f-43a5-aa14-745dc76bc670>.

9. EU favourability is down. There has been a double-digit drop in France (down 17 percentage points) and Spain (16 points), and single-digit declines in Germany (8 points), the United Kingdom (7 points), and Italy (6 points); see <www.pewglobal.org/2016/06/07/euroskepticism-beyond-brexit/>.

See also www.pewglobal.org/2013/05/13/the-new-sick-man-of-europe-the-european-union/>.

10. Ralf Dahrendorf, *Reflections on the Revolution in Europe* (London: Times Books, 1990), 30.

11. Peter Dauvergne and Genevieve LeBaron, *Protest Inc.: The Corporatization of Activism* (Cambridge: Polity, 2014).

12. Friedrich A. Hayek, *The Road to Serfdom* (Chicago: University of Chicago Press, 1944).

13. <www.theguardian.com/books/2014/aug/29/socialism-for-the-rich>. See also Owen Jones, *The Establishment: And How They Get Away With It* (London: Allen Lane, 2014).

14. Thomas Piketty, *Capital in the Twenty-First Century* (Cambridge, MA: Belknap, 2014).

15. <www.theguardian.com/books/2016/apr/15/neoliberalism-ideology- problem-george-monbiot>.

16. Susan Strange, *Casino Capitalism* (Manchester: Manchester University Press, 1997).

17. Naomi Klein, *The Shock Doctrine: Rise of Disaster Capitalism* (London: Allen Lane, 2007).

18. Paul Verhaeghe documents that neo-liberal economics is responsible for epidemics of self-harm, eating disorders, depression, loneliness, performance anxiety and social phobia. See Paul Verhaeghe and Jane Hedley-Prôle, *What about Me?: The Struggle for Identity in a Market-based Society* (Victoria, Australia, and London: Scribe, 2014).

19. <www.project-syndicate.org/commentary/globalization-new-discontents-by-joseph-e–stiglitz-2016-08>.

20. <www.imf.org/external/pubs/cat/longres.aspx?sk=41291>.

21. In the UK all three major political parties receive financial support from representatives of big business. This does not mean, however, that the relationship between political parties and the business community is straightforward. For details see <www.ft.com/content/70295a84-c4f4-11e5-b3b1-7b2481276e45>.

22. <www.theguardian.com/books/2016/apr/15/neoliberalism-ideology- problem-george-monbiot>.

23. <www.oecd-ilibrary.org/economics/income-inequality-in-the-european-union_5k9bdt47q5zt-en>.

24. See e.g. Maja Kluger Rasmussen, 'The Battle for Influence: The Politics of Business Lobbying in the European Parliament, The Impact of the Welfare State on Support for Europe', *Journal of Common Market Studies*, 53/2 (2015).

25. <www.independent.co.uk/news/uk/politics/theresa-may-speech-tory- confer ence-2016-in-full-transcript-a7346171.html>.

26. As Fraser Nelson put it a few months after May's speech: 'Mrs May has shown a quality relatively rare in politicians: the ability to change her mind. Almost all of her bad ideas have been quietly abandoned. Interfering with company boards? No longer. A pay cap? An idea dropped so quickly it didn't have time to leak,' <www.telegraph.co.uk/news/2017/01/19/evolu tion-theresa-may-sets-brexit-britain-course-bright-global/>.

27. <www.europarl.europa.eu/sides/getDoc.do?pubRef=-//EP//TEXT+CRE+20161214 +ITEM-007+DOC+XML+V0//EN&language=en&query=INTERV&detail= 3-023-000>. In the end, Pittella lost the contest to Antonio Tajani, <www.economist.com/news/europe/21715024-antonio-tajani-has-shaky-coalition-and-daunting-agenda-european-parliaments-new-president>.

28. Wolfgang Streeck, *Buying Time: The Delayed Crisis of Democratic Capitalism* (London: Verso, 2014), 45–6.

29. Paul Mason, *Postcapitalism: A Guide to Our Future* (London: Penguin 2016).

Chapter 5

1. Zygmunt Bauman, *Liquid Fear* (Cambridge: Polity, 2006), 2.

2. Marine Le Pen, cited in Aurelien Bredeen, 'Paris Attacks: The violence, its victims and how the investigation unfolded', *New York Times*, 14 November 2015, <www.nytimes.com/live/paris-attacks-live-updates/le-pen-the-french-are-no-longer-safe/>.

3. Marine Le Pen, cited in Gregory Viscusi and Alexandre Boksenbaum-Granier, 'French Unity Cracks as Opposition Slams Nice Security Response', *Bloomberg*, 15 July 2016, <www.bloomberg.com/news/articles/2016-07-15/attack-in-nice-draws-barbs-from-opposition-after-year-of-silence>.

4. Timothy Garton Ash, 'Germany's Choice', *Foreign Affairs*, 73/4 (1994), 65.

5. Robert Kagan, *Paradise and Power: America and Europe in the New World Order* (London: Atlantic Books, 2004), paperback edn., 3 and 5.

6. *Wider Europe—Neighbourhood: A New Framework for Relations with our Eastern and Southern Neighbours*, Communication from the Commission to the Council and the European Parliament (Brussels, 11.3.2003), COM (2003) 104 final. See also Council conclusions, 'Wider Europe—New Neighbourhood', available at <www.consilium.europa.eu/en/european-council/conclusions/1993-2003/>, Thessaloniki, 19–20 June 2003.

7. In April 2016, after eight years of frustrating negotiations, the European Commission proposed to the Council of the European Union and the

European Parliament that visa requirements be lifted for the citizens of Ukraine, but a year later this proposal has not yet been implemented. See <http://ec.europa.eu/home-affairs/what-is-new/news/news/2016/20160420_3_en>.

8. Nick Witney and Susi Dennison, 'Europe's Neighbourhood: Crisis as the New Normal', ECFR Policy Memo, London 2015, 1, <www.ecfr.eu/publica tions/summary/europes_neighbourhood_crisis_as_the_new_normal>.

9. 'Reviewing the European Neighbourhood Policy: Eastern Perspectives', ed. Alina Inayeh and Jörg Forbrig, *Europe Policy Paper*, 4 (Washington DC: German Marshall Fund of the United States, 2015), 1. See also Ana E. Juncos and Richard G. Whitman, 'Europe as a Regional Actor: Neighbourhood Lost?' *Journal of Common Market Studies*, 2015, <http://onlinelibrary. wiley.com/journal/10.1111/(ISSN)1468-5965/earlyview>.

10. 'Few other European politicians have had the courage to make such a clear link between Europe's values, its collective self-interest and bold action on refugees…In a crisis where Europe has little to be proud of, Mrs. Merkel's leadership is a shining exception,' commented *The Economist*. See 'Merkel the bold', *The Economist*, 5 September 2015, <www.economist.com/news/lead ers/21663228-refugees-germanys-chancellor-brave-decisive-and-right-merkel-bold>.

11. See an interview with Ulrich Beck, <http://blogs.lse.ac.uk/europpblog/2013/ 03/25/five-minutes-with-ulrich-beck-germany-has-created-an-accidental-empire/>, and with George Soros, 'Remarks at the Festival of Economics', Trento, 2 June 2012, available at <www.georgesoros.com/interviews-speeches/ entry/ remarks_at_the_festival_of_economics_trento_italy/>.

12. Simon Heffer, 'Rise of the Fourth Reich, how Germany is using the financial crisis to conquer Europe', *Daily Mail*, 17 August 2011, <www.dailymail. co.uk/ news/article-2026840/European-debt-summit-Germany-using- financial-crisis-conquer-Europe.html>.

13. According to NATO's official document Russia's destabilizing actions and policies include: the ongoing illegal and illegitimate annexation of Crimea, which we do not and will not recognize and which we call on Russia to reverse; the violation of sovereign borders by force; the deliberate destabilization of eastern Ukraine; large-scale snap exercises contrary to the spirit of the Vienna Document, and provocative military activities near NATO borders, including in the Baltic and Black Sea regions and the Eastern Mediterranean; its irresponsible and aggressive nuclear rhetoric, military concept, and underlying posture; and its repeated violations of NATO Allied airspace. In addition, Russia's military intervention, significant military presence and support for the regime in Syria, and its use of its

military presence in the Black Sea to project power into the Eastern Mediterranean have posed further risks and challenges for the security of Allies and others. See *Warsaw Summit Communiqué* issued by the Heads of State and Government participating in the meeting of the North Atlantic Council in Warsaw, 8–9 July 2016, <www.nato.int/cps/en/natohq/official_texts_133169.htm?selectedLocale=en>.

14. <www.welt.de/politik/deutschland/article161766668/Deutsche-verlieren-wegen-Trump-Vertrauen-in-die-USA.html>.
15. See <www.beppegrillo.it/2013/02/la_iii_guerra_mondiale_e_in_corso.html>.
16. Zygmunt Bauman, *Liquid Fear* (Cambridge: Polity, 2006), 2.
17. See Ruth Forsyth, 'Russia's Hybrid Warfare is Harming Germany', *Atlantic Council*, 12 May 2016, <www.atlanticcouncil.org/blogs/natosource/russia-s-hybrid-warfare-is-harming-germany>.
18. MAD used to refer to Mutually Assured (nuclear) Destruction. See Mark Leonard, *Connectivity Wars* (London: European Council on Foreign Relations, 2016), <www.ecfr.eu/europeanpower/geoeconomics>.
19. Georg Sørensen, *Rethinking the New World Order* (London: Palgrave, 2016), 5.
20. <www.foreignaffairs.com/articles/world/2017-04-17/liberal-order-rigged?cid=int-now&pgtype=hpg&region=br1>.
21. See <www.theguardian.com/politics/blog/live/2016/jul/18/trident-debate-renewal-corbyn-may-idealism-as-mps-prepare-for-trident-vote-politics-live>.
22. See <www.usnews.com/news/world/articles/2016-07-08/the-latest-german-defense-minister-backs-border-force>.
23. See <www.france24.com/en/20160812-french-mayor-bans-full-body-burkinis-cannes-beaches-muslim-burqa>. Also <www.theguardian.com/world/2016/aug/19/german-interior-minister-backs-burqa-bans-public-places>.
24. T. S. Eliot, 'The Love Song of J. Alfred Prufrock', in *The Waste Land and Other Poems* (New York: Harvest, 1930). Reproduced with permission of Faber and Faber Ltd.

Chapter 6

1. Wei Yuan, cited in William Pfaff, *Barbarian Sentiments* (New York: Hill & Wang, 2000), cover page.
2. In 1992 the EU received 672,000 asylum seekers, and numbers remained high during the Bosnia conflict. In 2001 numbers again peaked at 424,000 following the Kosovo crisis and with many arriving from Somalia and Afghanistan. In 2015 numbers exceeded those figures but not dramatically, especially when one considers that in 1992 there were fifteen EU member

states and currently there are twenty-eight. For detailed statistics see <http://ec.europa.eu/eurostat/statistics-explained/index.php/asylum_statistics>.

3. Franck Duvell, 'Quo Vadis Europe?', in Edit Andras et al. (eds.), *Vienna Festival Open Forum Catalogue* (Vienna: Universal Hospitality, 2016), 11–13.

4. <www.youtube.com/watch?v=RIDOMHym7p4>.

5. Victor Orbán's interview for *Politico* on 23 November 2015, <www.politico.eu/article/viktor-orban-interview-terrorists-migrants-eu-russia-putin-borders-schengen/>.

6. Alexander Betts, *Survival Migration: Failed Governance and the Crisis of Displacement* (Ithaca, NY: Cornell University Press, 2013).

7. See data cited in Maeve Glavey, 'Immigration fears: a vulnerable public in the face of change', *Policy Network*, September 2016, <www.policy-network.net/pno_detail.aspx?ID=6130&title=Immigration-fears-a-vulnerable-public-in-the-face-of-change>.

8. <www.rt.com/news/france-eu-immigrants-pen/>.

9. The rapid increase in EU workers—700,000 extra in 2012–15—coincided with an increase of one million British people in work. See data provided by <www.independent.co.uk/news/uk/politics/eu-referendum-immigration-and-brexit-what-lies-have-been-spread-a7092521.html>.

10. EU member states which utilized a seven-year transition period for preparing social service ahead of the new labour influx have experienced much less political anxiety about working Poles and other East Europeans than was the case in Great Britain. Bela Galgoczi, Janine Leschke, and Andrew Watt, *EU Labour Migration in Troubled Times: Skills Mismatch, Return and Policy Responses* (London: Routledge, 2012).

11. <www.theguardian.com/commentisfree/2016/mar/18/migration-leaders-david-cameron-refugees-libya-movement-of-people>.

12. <www.theguardian.com/uk-news/2013/jul/26/go-home-ad-campaign-court-challenge>.

13. <http://visegradrevue.eu/thursday-21st-century-europe/>.

Chapter 7

1. Mark Leonard, *Why Europe Will Run the 21st Century* (London: HarperCollins, 2005).

2. <http://foreignpolicy.com/2017/04/13/europe-is-still-a-superpower/>.

3. John Stuart Mill, *Principles of Political Economy* (New York: Prometheus Books, 2004), originally published by John W. Parker in 1848. For a more detailed

analysis see Katherine Barbieri, *The Liberal Illusion: Does Trade Promote Peace?* (Ann Arbor: University of Michigan Press, 2002).

4. <https://europa.eu/european-union/about-eu/symbols/europe-day/schuman-declaration_en>.

5. <www.cvce.eu/content/publication/1999/1/1/0c817dc4-c498-4b7d-9e67-a096711d98b0/publishable_en.pdf>.

6. For the official results of the elections see <www.europarl.europa.eu/elections2014-results/en/election-results-2014.html>.

7. Reported by the BBC on 26 May 2014, <www.bbc.com/news/world-europe-27559714>.

8. Juncker served as the first permanent President of the Eurogroup responsible for handling the crisis and his secretive, deceptive, and unscrupulous style of handling the crisis has gained him a nickname: 'master of lies'. Criticism of Juncker has intensified after it was revealed that 340 multinationals may have used Luxembourg for tax evasion. Juncker denied any complicity in these operations but admitted his political responsibility for what he described as 'excessive tax engineering'. See 'Europe's big tax scam', ECFR, 17 November 2014, <www.ecfr.eu/article/commentary_europes_big_tax_scam350>. Also Leigh Phillips, 'Attacks mount against "master of lies" Juncker', *EU Observer*, 10 May 2011, <https://euobserver.com/economic/32294>.

9. Interview with Donald Tusk, *Polityka*, 3–9 December 2014, p. 21. See also his interview for *Rzeczpospolita* on 16 July 2015.

10. See e.g. Amie Kreppel, *The European Parliament and Supranational Party System* (Cambridge: Cambridge University Press, 2002), 215–23, and Simon Hix, 'Party Politics in the European Union', in Henrik Enderlein, Sonja Wälti, and Michael Zürn (eds.), *Handbook on Multi-Level Governance* (Cheltenham: Edward Elgar, 2011), 227–38.

11. <www.socialeurope.eu/2017/04/rome-declaration-union-not-state/>.

12. <https://yougov.co.uk/news/2016/06/27/how-britain-voted/>.

13. <www.bbc.co.uk/news/uk-scotland-scotland-politics-36599102>.

14. <www.telegraph.co.uk/news/2017/04/03/nothing-wrong-britain-playing-mr-nasty-negotiating-brexit/>; see also <www.politico.eu/article/france-plan-for-a-bloody-brexit-eu-referendum-consequences-europe-hollande-david-cameron/>.

15. <www.thetimes.co.uk/edition/comment/compulsory-voting-can-make-britain-fairer-swq077k8w?CMP=Sprkr-_-Editorial-_-thetimes-_- Comment andOpinion-_-Cardkitandlink-_-Statement-_-Unspecified-_- ACCOUNT_ TYPE&linkId=36262526>.

16. <www.independent.co.uk/news/uk/politics/brexit-poll-leave-voters-death-penalty-yougov-results-light-bulbs-a7656791.html>.

17. In the so-called Pact of Amsterdam adopted in 2016 the EU has launched its Urban Agenda. The Pact has recognized cities as vital actors, but it has not granted them any formal powers within the EU. See <http://ec.europa.eu/regional_policy/sources/policy/themes/urban-development/agenda/pact-of-amsterdam.pdf>.

Chapter 8

1. Franco 'Bifo' Berardi, Gary Genosko, and Nicholas Thoburn (eds.), *After the Future* (Edinburgh: AK Press, 2011), and 'The Future has no Future', in *The Invisible Committee, The Coming Insurrection* (Los Angeles: Semiotext(e), 2009), 23.

2. <www.iwm.at/files/IWMpost_111.pdf>.

3. <www.famous-quotes-and-quotations.com/yogi-berra-quotes.html>. For a scientific take on the topic see Gerald Schneider, Nils Petter Gleditsch, and Sabine Carey, 'Forecasting in International Relations. One Quest, Three Approaches', *Conflict Management and Peace Science*, 28/1 (2011), 5–14.

4. Zygmunt Bauman, *Liquid Times: Living in an Age of Uncertainty* (Cambridge: Polity, 2007), 97. Kołakowski observed that Utopias not only strive for non-existing objects, but also that Utopian objects are pregnant with unsolvable contradictions. See Leszek Kołakowski, *Modernity on Endless Trial* (Chicago: University of Chicago Press, 1991).

5. Karl Popper, *The Open Society and Its Enemies* (London: Routledge, 1945), i and ii.

6. Ralf Dahrendorf. *Reflections on the Revolution in Europe* (London: Times Books, 1990), 26.

7. John Gray, *Isaiah Berlin* (London: HarperCollins, 1995), 43. John A. Hall pointed to other tensions within liberalism, such as between wealth and freedom and between knowledge and morality. John A. Hall, *Liberalism: Politics, Ideology and the Market* (London: Paladin, 1987), 2.

8. Karl R. Popper, *The Open Society and Its Enemies* (London: Routledge,1945), i. 1.

9. Bauman, *Liquid Times*, 6.

10. Ibid. 7.

11. Ibid.

12. This is not to idealize cities, of course. Cities may well be seen as places inspiring new technological applications, creative lifestyles, or business experiments, but they are also sites of exploitation, ethno-racial discrimination, and

environmental degradation. See Ugo Rossi, *Cities in Global Capitalism* (Cambridge: Polity, 2017).

13. Kate Raworth, *Doughnut Economics: Seven Ways to Think Like a 21st-Century Economist* (London: Penguin, 2017).

14. The Bolshevik Revolution to overthrow capitalism started with an assault on the Winter Palace in St Petersburg on 25 October 1917. See Sheila Fitzpatrick, *The Russian Revolution* (Oxford: Oxford University Press, 2008), 61–7.

15. Paul Mason, *Postcapitalism: A Guide to Our Future* (London: Penguin, 2016), p. xvi.

16. I spelled out these ideas in *Is the EU Doomed?* (Cambridge: Polity, 2014), 92–114.

17. David Beetham, *Parliament and Democracy in the Twenty-First Century: A Guide to Good Practice* (Geneva: Inter-Parliamentary Union), 2006.

18. Nadia Urbinati, 'Representative Democracy and its Critics', in Sonia Alonso, John Keane, and Wolfgang Merkel (eds.), *The Future of Representative Democracy* (Cambridge: Cambridge University Press, 2011), 23. Also Nadia Urbinati, *Representative Democracy: Principles and Genealogy* (Chicago: Chicago University Press, 2006).

19. Giovanni Sartori, 'Video-Power', *Government and Opposition*, 24/1 (1989), 39–40. See also Benjamin Barber, *Strong Democracy: Participatory Politics for a New Age* (Berkeley, CA: University of California Press, 1994).

20. Saskia Sassen, 'Local Actors in Global Politics', *Current Sociology*, 52/4 (2004), 649–70.

21. John Keane, 'Monitory Democracy?' in Sonia Alonso, John Keane, and Wolfgang Merkel (eds.), *The Future of Representative Democracy* (Cambridge: Cambridge University Press, 2011), 213. Also John Keane, *Democracy and Media Decadence* (Cambridge: Cambridge University Press, 2013).

22. Stephen Coleman, *Can the Internet Strengthen Democracy?* (Cambridge: Polity, 2017), 1.

23. Phillip Pettit, *Republicanism* (Oxford: Oxford University Press, 1999), 183–205.

24. Mason, *Postcapitalism*, p. xvii.

25. Helen Margetts, Peter John, Scott Halle, and Taha Yasseri, *Political Turbulence: How Social Media Shape Collective Action* (Princeton: Princeton University Press, 2016), 206. Also Cass R. Sustein, *Republic.com.2.0* (Princeton: Princeton University Press, 2007).

26. Manuel Castells, *The Internet Galaxy: Reflections on the Internet, Business, and Society* (Oxford: Oxford University Press, 2001), 133.

27. Owen Jones, *Chavs: The Demonization of the Working Class* (London: Verso, 2011), 4.

28. Ralf Dahrendorf, *Class and Class Conflict in Industrial Society* (London: Routledge, 1959), first published in German by Ferdinand Enke in 1957.

29. Dahrendorf, *Reflections*, 153–4.

30. Ibid. 154.

31. Ralf Dahrendorf, 'Der Intellektuelle und die Gesellschaft', *Die Zeit*, 29 March 1963.

FURTHER READING

This section contains a selection of books that may help the reader to explore some of the topics discussed in this letter. Choices made are personal and therefore highly biased, and they are all in English which is a serious limitation. However, I hope the selected books offer an appetizing intellectual menu. Enjoy your reading!

Dahrendorf

After 1989: Morals, Revolution and Civil Society (Basingstoke: Macmillan, 1997).

Reflections on the Revolution in Europe (New York, Times Books, 1990).

The Modern Social Conflict. An Essay on the Politics of Liberty (London: Weidenfeld & Nicolson, 1988).

Essays in the Theory of Society (Stanford, CA: Stanford University Press, 1968).

Conflict after Class: New Perspectives on the Theory of Social and Political Conflict (London: Longmans, 1967).

Class and Class Conflict in Industrial Society (London: Routledge & Kegan Paul, 1957).

Liberalism

Isaiah Berlin, *Liberty* (Oxford: Oxford University Press, 2002).

Friedrich A. Hayek, *The Constitution of Liberty* (Chicago: Chicago University Press, 1960).

Michael Freeden, *Liberalism: A Very Short Introduction* (Oxford: Oxford University Press, 2015).

John Gray, *Two Faces of Liberalism* (New York: The New Press, 2000).

Amartya Sen, *Development as Freedom* (Oxford: Oxford University Press, 1999).

Karl Popper, *The Open Society and Its Enemies* (London: Routledge, 1945).

Anti-liberalism

Toril Aalberg, Frank Esser, Carsten Reinemann, Jesper Stromback, and Claes De Vreese (eds.), *Populist Political Communication in Europe* (London: Routledge, 2017).

Cas Mudde, *On Extremism and Democracy in Europe* (London: Routledge, 2016).

Jan Werner-Müller, *What is Populism?* (Philadelphia: University of Pennsylvania Press, 2016).

Stephen Holmes, *The Anatomy of Antiliberalism* (Cambridge, MA: Harvard University Press, 1993).

Jacob Leib Talmon, *The Origins of Totalitarian Democracy* (London: Secker & Warburg, 1960).

Hannah Arendt, *The Origins of Totalitarianism* (New York: Schocken, 1951).

Post-Liberalism

Bill Emmott, *The Fate of the West: The Battle to Save the World's Most Successful Political Idea* (London: Profile Books, 2017).

Ivan Krastev, *After Europe* (Philadelphia: Pennsylvania University Press, 2017).

Edward Luce, *The Retreat of Western Liberalism* (London: Little, Brown, 2017).

Saskia Sassen, *Expulsions: Brutality and Complexity in the Global Economy* (Cambridge, MA: Harvard University Press, 2014).

David Marquand, *The End of the West: The Once and Future Europe* (Princeton: Princeton University Press, 2011).

Georg Sørensen, *A Liberal World Order in Crisis* (Ithaca: Cornell University Press, 2011).

Democracy

John Keane, *Democracy and Media Decadence* (Cambridge: Cambridge University Press, 2013).

Peter Mair, *Ruling the Void* (London: Verso, 2013).

Pierre Rosanvallon, *Counter-Democracy: Politics in an Age of Distrust* (Cambridge: Cambridge University Press, 2008).

Nadia Urbinati, *Representative Democracy: Principles and Genealogy* (Chicago: Chicago University Press, 2006).

Larry Diamond and Leonardo Morlino (eds.), *Assessing the Quality of Democracy* (Baltimore, MA: Johns Hopkins University Press, 2005).

Colin Crouch, *Post-Democracy* (Cambridge: Polity, 2004).

Capitalism

Jürgen Kocka, *Capitalism: A Short History* (Princeton, NJ: Princeton University Press, 2016).

Wolfgang Streeck, *How Will Capitalism End?: Essays on a Failing System* (London: Verso, 2016).

Naomi Klein, *This Changes Everything: Capitalism vs. the Climate* (New York: Simon & Schuster, 2014).

Michael J. Sandel, *What Money Can't Buy: The Moral Limits of Markets* (New York: Farrar, Straus & Giroux, 2012).

Dani Rodrik, *The Globalization Paradox* (Oxford: Oxford University Press, 2011).

Milton Friedman, *Capitalism and Freedom: Fortieth Anniversary Edition* (Chicago: Chicago University Press, 2002).

Borders

Christian Joppke, *Is Multiculturalism Dead? Crisis and Persistence in the Constitutional State* (Cambridge: Polity, 2017).

Andrew Geddes and Peter Scholten, *The Politics of Migration and Immigration in Europe* (London: Sage, 2016).

Charles S. Maier, *Once Within Borders: Territories of Power, Wealth, and Belonging since 1500* (Cambridge, MA: Harvard University Press, 2016).

Christopher Hill, *Foreign Policy: Home Truths* (Cambridge: Cambridge University Press, 2014).

Saskia Sassen, *Territory, Authority and Rights. From Medieval to Global Assemblages* (Princeton, NJ: Princeton University Press, 2006).

James Rosenau, *Along the Domestic-Foreign Frontier: Exploring Governance in a Turbulent World* (Cambridge: Cambridge University Press, 1997).

Geopolitics

Parag Khanna, *Connectography: Mapping the Future of Global Civilization* (New York: Random House, 2016).

Mark Leonard (ed.), *Connectivity Wars: Why Migration, Finance and Trade are the Geo-Economic Battle Grounds of the Future* (London: European Council on Foreign Relations, 2016).

Henry Kissinger, *World Order* (New York: Penguin, 2014).

Robert D. Kaplan, *The Revenge of Geography: What the Map Tells Us About Coming Conflicts and the Battle Against Fate* (New York: Random House, 2012).

Noel Parker (ed.), *The Geopolitics of Europe's Identity: Centers, Boundaries, and Margins* (Basingstoke: Palgrave, 2008).

Monica Duffy Toft, *The Geography of Ethnic Violence: Identity, Interests, and the Indivisibility of Territory* (Princeton, NJ: Princeton University Press, 2003).

Power

Ulrich Beck, *German Europe* (Cambridge: Polity, 2013).

Manuel Castells, *Communication Power* (Cambridge: Polity, 2013).

Joseph S. Nye Jr., *The Future of Power* (New York: Public Affairs, 2011).

Paul Hirst, *Space and Power: Politics, War and Architecture* (Cambridge: Polity, 2005).

Steven Lukes, *Power: A Radical View* (Basingstoke: Palgrave, 2004).

Dominic Lieven, *Empire: The Russian Empire and its Rivals* (New Haven, CT: Yale University Press, 2001).

Integration

Chris Bickerton, *The European Union: A Citizen's Guide* (London: Pelican, 2016).
Harold James, *Making the European Monetary Union* (Cambridge, MA: Harvard University Press, 2012).
Stefano Bartolini, *Restructuring Europe: Centre Formation, System Building, and Political Structuring between the Nation State and the European Union* (Oxford: Oxford University Press, 2007).
Fritz Scharpf, *Governing in Europe: Effective and Democratic?* (Oxford: Oxford University Press, 1999).
Andrew Moravcsik, *The Choice for Europe: Social Purpose and State Power from Messina to Maastricht* (Ithaca, NY: Cornell University Press, 1998).
Alan Milward, *The European Rescue of the Nation State* (London: Routledge, 1992).

Crisis

Joseph E. Stiglitz, *The Euro: How a Common Currency Threatens the Future of Europe* (New York: Allen Lane, 2016).
Loukas Tsoukalis, *In Defence of Europe: Can the European Project Be Saved?* (Oxford: Oxford University Press, 2016).
Erik Jones, *The Year the European Crisis Ended* (Basingstoke: Palgrave/Macmillan, 2014).
Giandomenico Majone, *Rethinking the Union of Europe Post-Crisis: Has Integration Gone Too Far?* (Cambridge: Cambridge University Press, 2014).
Anthony Giddens, *Turbulent and Mighty Continent: What Future for Europe?* (Cambridge: Polity, 2013).
Jürgen Habermas, *The Crisis of the European Union: A Response* (Cambridge: Polity, 2012).

History

Brendan Simms, *Europe: The Struggle for Supremacy, 1453 to the Present* (London: Penguin, 2013).
Perry Anderson, *The New Old World* (London: Verso, 2011).
Tony Judt, *Post-War: A History of Europe Since 1945* (New York: Penguin, 2005).
Mark Mazower, *Dark Continent: Europe's Twentieth Century* (New York: Allen Lane, 1998).
Charles S. Maier, *Dissolution: The Crisis of Communism and the End of East Germany* (Princeton, NJ: Princeton University Press, 1997).
Norman Davies, *Europe: A History* (Oxford: Oxford University Press, 1996).

INDEX